Happiest Mom
ON THE
Block

THE GREATEST GIFT WE CAN GIVE
OUR CHILDREN IS OUR HAPPINESS

KATERINA MAYANTS

BALBOA.
PRESS
A DIVISION OF HAY HOUSE

Balboa Press books may be ordered through booksellers or by contacting:

Balboa Press
A Division of Hay House
1663 Liberty Drive
Bloomington, IN 47403
www.balboapress.com
1 (877) 407-4847

Because of the dynamic nature of the Internet, any web addresses or links contained in this book may have changed since publication and may no longer be valid. The views expressed in this work are solely those of the author and do not necessarily reflect the views of the publisher, and the publisher hereby disclaims any responsibility for them.

The author of this book does not dispense medical advice or prescribe the use of any technique as a form of treatment for physical, emotional, or medical problems without the advice of a physician, either directly or indirectly. The intent of the author is only to offer information of a general nature to help you in your quest for emotional and spiritual well-being. In the event you use any of the information in this book for yourself, which is your constitutional right, the author and the publisher assume no responsibility for your actions.

Any people depicted in stock imagery provided by Thinkstock are models, and such images are being used for illustrative purposes only.
Certain stock imagery © Thinkstock.

Print information available on the last page.

ISBN: 978-1-5043-6918-3 (sc)
ISBN: 978-1-5043-6919-0 (hc)
ISBN: 978-1-5043-6917-6 (e)

Library of Congress Control Number: 2016918033

Balboa Press rev. date: 12/20/2016

Introduction

I was born in Gomel, Belarus, on February 15, 1983, during one of the biggest blizzards in Belarus history. No worries; I was nice and toasty, snuggled next to my mother, who wanted nothing more than to have a baby girl. My older brother, Max, was five when he met me for the first time. He loves telling me the story of "the greatest day" of his life—the day he got to hold my tiny six-pound body and look in my sleepy blue eyes. My father, to this day, recalls my birth as the day he melted in love. No doubt I was deeply loved and truly wanted.

Growing up in Communist Russia is similar to a bird growing up in a cage; it's hard to know the difference between perceived freedom and actual freedom. I was a happy child, though I often wondered about my last name.

"Mama, why we do we have your last name and not Papa's?" I asked innocently around the age of six.

"Well, my last name is Russian, and Papa's is Jewish. It's safer this way for us all," she replied, without further explanation.

Truth is, my father had very few opportunities in Belarus (formerly part of the Soviet Union) as a Jewish man during the Communist regime.. He was limited to working either in music or in a factory. One day, I came home, and there was a swastika drawn on our front door. Someone got word in my brother's school that we had a Jewish father and decided to take out their hate for Jews on our door. I don't remember what happened in the weeks after this horrific event, but my parents kept going back and forth to Leningrad (now Saint Petersburg).

In January 1991, a coffin–like box arrived at our house. My mother explained it was the box that would transport all of our belongings to America. I was confused. "Wait—we're going to America?" I asked.

"Yes, where Michael Jackson lives and Disney World is!" my mother said, trying desperately to seem enthusiastic. Well, she said the magic words: Michael Jackson, my favorite artist, and Disney World, a place I thought only existed in heaven.

On January 25, 1991, we arrived in New York City. I had my favorite doll in one arm and our little dog in the other. Life was confusing but so exciting—a new country, a new beginning, a new place to call home. The first few months were both exciting and scary at the same time. Learning a new language was hard, but tasting a banana for the first time was amazing! I had my eighth birthday just three weeks after we arrived, and all my cousins who lived in America came to celebrate with me. I was in awe of their ability to speak English and Russian flawlessly, and I wanted to be just like them.

I started second grade shortly after my birthday, and I met the very first black person I'd ever known. She seemed so different at first—her lips were larger than mine, and her hair was nothing like my hair, never mind our skin-color difference. But after a few days of sharing a desk, we got to know each other through the little English I knew at the time. Over the next few months, we became good friends, and she began to look very similar to me, not as foreign, as I once perceived her. We learned in class about different cultures from around the world, and I was so excited to be in a country that had so much diversity. My parents and brother, on the other hand, didn't receive the same education I did, and so they isolated themselves from anyone who wasn't Russian because of their fear of someone's unknown culture.

My parents insisted that we speak English at home because it was the language of the country we now called home. If we wanted to make it, we'd have to become Americanized. I spent many years watching *Full House* on TV and learning English from the simple language style of the show. My answer to almost everything was, "You got it, dude," which I said while giving a thumbs-up.

Money was tight, and my parents worked two jobs each to make ends meet, though I never really felt a lack of anything. I was happy with my color-changing pen that I got for Christmas one year. We lived in a decent apartment in a nice neighborhood. I loved saving plastic 7-Up bottles and taking them to the plastic-crushing machines at our local grocery store for five cents a bottle. I didn't realize I was surrounded by the homeless people in our town. I thought everyone crushed bottles for fun, especially when it meant I could buy an individually wrapped Jolly Rancher candy, which, amazingly, was five cents. It wasn't until I witnessed my parents arguing over money and stressing almost to the point of tears that I understood our dire situation. Money became my enemy, the main source of so much sorrow for my family.

If it wasn't for money, we would be happy, I thought. *I hate it. I wish it didn't exist. My parents wouldn't argue, and my mom wouldn't cry.* I didn't realize at the time, but these moments of pain, powerlessness, and desperation would shape my belief system toward money for much of my adult life.

When I was eleven, my parents enrolled me in a *yeshiva* (Jewish school). That is where my entire understanding of life began to change. I learned about the Torah and of all the stories of our forefathers. Every day in fourth and fifth grade, I sat at my desk and took notes on all I was learning. One day, I realized it was not resonating with me. "Mrs. Titlebow," I said to my teacher, "I have a question. Why can't we rip toilet paper, turn on the lights, or carry anything in our pockets on Shabbos [the Sabbath]?" The whole class gasped in shock, for I was the first girl to ask questions of the teachings.

"Good question," answered the teacher. "All the things you

mentioned are work. You can't do work on Shabbos; it's a time of rest."

I was still confused, as ripping toilet paper and turning on the lights didn't seem like much work to me as much as a daily thoughtless occurrence. The teacher started to move on, but I raised my hand. She took a deep breath and called on me.

"I have another question. If I wear a dress that covers my knees and elbows on a very hot summer day, is every drop of sweat that comes off my body considered a *mitzvah* [good deed] that brings me closer to getting in to heaven?"

At this point the teacher was running out of patience, but she still answered with a polite yes.

It was at that moment in fifth grade that I realized what a bunch of bullshit all this religion is. I understood—not in my mind but in my heart—that God just wants us to be happy and kind, to be the best versions of ourselves, not our drops of sweat or our fully resting on Shabbos. He doesn't care if we rip a piece of toilet paper or carry keys in our pockets on Saturdays. All this was some sort of human-control idea that was so far away from God's will for us to be aware of who we are and give back to the world the best of ourselves. I told my parents I was no longer willing to get brainwashed by the zombie-like teachers and asked to be transferred to a public school. It was during this time in my life that I began to question everything that didn't feel right, and I haven't stopped since.

One of the most profound moments that shaped my understanding of what a woman should be happened when I was fourteen. I met a boy who was very tall, with striking blue eyes and blond hair. He was funny and confident, and I instantly fell in love with him. Though he had a girlfriend, I was happy just to be around him. I would watch for what this "ideal boy" wanted in an "ideal girlfriend" by observing his relationships. One day, we were sitting in his house, listening to music, and his pager went off. It was his girlfriend. He ignored her page, but a few minutes later she paged him again.

"Ugh, why can't she leave me alone?" he moaned. "Why is she always nagging me?"

At that moment, as a very raw and easily molded teen, I made a mental note that read, *Don't nag, don't page, and don't expect a call back. He'll call when he feels like it.* A few moments later, his mom walked in the room and handed him the house phone.

"Yel-low," he said, trying to be cool. It was his girlfriend, of course, and she was very angry with him. I could hear her screaming.

"If I page you, you call me back! That's why you have a pager. Not when you feel like it but when I page you. If you don't want to speak to me, then let me know, and I will move on. I don't want to play these games anymore." And she hung up.

"What a bitch. What a nagging, annoying bitch," he said, with the phone still in his hand.

I made more mental notes: *Don't be a bitch, don't make demands, and don't expect a call back immediately. But more important, don't be annoying.*

The very next day, "Dream Boy" and his girlfriend joined my friends for pizza. Dream Boy said something about her eating too much pizza and that he feared she would get fat. She stood up and looked him dead in the eyes. In front of everyone. she said, "How dare you talk to me that way? Who do you think you are? No one ever talks to me like that."

Everyone was silent but Dream Boy said, "God, what a bitch she is. She always makes so much drama out of everything. So annoying; so embarrassing."

I added to my mental notes, titled "Dream Girlfriend": *Don't say anything, stay quiet, and don't make a big deal out of things. Don't embarrass anyone, even if that person embarrasses you. Just don't be a bitch; be nice.*

I don't really remember how Dream Boy and I stopped being friends, but I remember every single mental note I made in the short time he was my one and only. The truth is I developed "Nice Girl syndrome," which has plagued most of my relationships and almost cost me my marriage. I was a nice girl. I didn't expect much from my boyfriends, and I did whatever they wanted to do. I never caused a fight or complained. I stayed quiet, often emotionless, and my biggest drive in the relationship was to be liked. I did everything to be perfect, and that is how I destroyed all my relationships and possibly friendships.

I was a lifeless zombie who would focus on pleasing but not contribute much to the relationship. After a while, the guys would get bored and would break up with me. I would ask a million times, "Why? Why? What did I do?" And most of them would reply, "Nothing. You did nothing but please me. But who are you, and what do you like to do? Doesn't anything bother you? Don't you have any interests besides me?"

I didn't get it, and I felt confused by the wonderful relationships my "bitchy" girlfriends were experiencing. My confusion was fueled by my inability to understand the term *bitch*, as my only understanding of the word came from Dream Boy. To me, a bitch was a woman who was loud, who always expressed herself, who didn't take crap from anyone. And who demanded to be treated like a queen. Wait—why was that such a bad thing? Why were women who demanded more from their partners considered bitches? Why did women who spoke their minds and didn't give a shit about what anyone thought get such a bad rap?

I began to question my belief system, but it would be many more years before I fully understood the magnitude and horrific reality of "Nice Wife syndrome." I am sure I am not alone in suffering from this "disease," which causes us to please all but ourselves.

Chapter 1

The sun is beginning to set, and it floods our living room with golden rays of light. My favorite time of the day is finally here. James, my husband, is in the kitchen, fixing dinner. Milana, our six-year-old, is making us dinner in her play kitchen, tossing the food in the frying pan … and it all falls to the floor. Madelyn, our three-year-old, is gently singing to her four baby dolls, covering them with blankets as she puts them to sleep. Mason, seven months, is trying his hardest to stand on his own two feet for more than three seconds before falling on his tushy.

I am basking in the bliss that is the end of what once was a very long tunnel, a tunnel darker than I ever imagined. Now, this light is brighter than I ever thought it could be. As I sit here in my living room, watching my greatest gifts play, smile, and enjoy life, and the room is flooded with the light of the most magnificent sunset, I can't help but think back on all the horrific struggles I faced to get here.

I am Katerina Mayants, and I am sick of telling pretty lies. Here is my true story.

September 2005

I was twenty-two, and it was my first week at my first real job after graduating college. I couldn't fathom sitting in an office all day, so working as a life-insurance agent was my best-case scenario, as

I would be out in the field, free to make my own schedule. On my first day at the main office, a really hot guy with turquoise eyes who seemed to enjoy spending time at the gym suggested that our genes, if mixed together, would make for beautiful children. James—the hot guy—was everything I was not looking for in a boyfriend, but somehow, no matter how hard my logical mind tried to talk me out of responding to his flirtations, my body kept tingling with a sensation only felt when a soul is connecting to its mate. We couldn't bear to be apart for more than a few hours, and so James came up with a logical reason for his sleeping in my parents' basement a few times a week—his drive home was an hour and forty-five minutes, and he might fall asleep at the wheel after a long day at work. (Good one, right?) Every night we stayed up talking, and then I went upstairs to my room, and he went downstairs to sleep on the couch. Every day was going to be the day he left to go home, but every day he stayed. On the rare occasions when he did leave, seconds after I heard his car start I would get a text message that read "I miss you. I am addicted to you."

After two months of pretending to be friends but wanting nothing more than to be lovers, we came home from a bar one night, and I said, "You don't have to go to the basement tonight. Come upstairs with me." It was the night that solidified our future together. We began spending nights at his place at least four times a week. Since meeting James, all our conversations about our future and how it could be really empowered me to give my all in sales. We did compete with each other at work, but it was such a driving force for me to see my own true potential. When I was with him, I felt all the forces of love in the world run through my body. I'd only known him for months, but I felt like we'd been together for many lifetimes before this one.

As we would fall asleep, face-to-face in each other's arms, I could feel light permeate my body. I felt so light, so good, as if my soul already knew it was one with the person it had been longing for. When waking up in his embrace after only a few hours of sleep,

I felt so rested, so peaceful, and so energized. I'd never felt such a connection with another human being. I remember riding with him down the main road in our town, sitting in the passenger's seat and thinking, *This is where I want to be for the rest of my life—us driving together down the road of life, side by side.* The town we were driving through was a sleepy, rundown part of New Jersey that wasn't very attractive. But that day, I looked out the window and felt in complete awe of the beauty around me. I saw love in everything that surrounded us. All the angels in the world orchestrated a series of unusual events for us to be united at the perfect time and in the perfect place in our lives. Our conversations were always about our dreams of having a lot of kids and a beautiful house full of joy, laughter, and love. I wanted so badly to have children with James because he had so much to teach a child. We had huge dreams, and our imaginations ran wild with how our life would one day be, as long as were together.

One day my brother and I were walking into a grocery store when I suddenly felt an incredible feeling. I stopped my brother and said, "Oh, my God, Max. I am so in love with James. I swear he is the one I am going to marry. There is no other way." Max was eager to get the food shopping finished and didn't really respond.

Luckily, James felt exactly the same about me. We didn't waste any time; just six months after our initial meeting we moved in to a beautiful townhouse on the water in a sleepy, tiny town on the Jersey Shore. Life was amazing, and we couldn't get enough of each other—until we got enough of each other and learned our differences. Truth is we came from two different worlds. I came from a Russian family and was taught that family is a part of every single decision. My parents and brother wouldn't let me make a move until I ran it by them and got their approval. My family was a part of everything I did. Our get-togethers were loud, and everyone had an opinion.

James, on the other hand, came from an American family. His parents got divorced when he was fifteen, and their involvement in his life was miniscule. It wasn't that they weren't tight, but he was raised to make his own decisions and fend for himself. Their family get-togethers were quiet, and no one really expressed opinions on anything; they just reminisced or talked of football.

When we decided to move in together, James didn't have to ask for permission from anyone, but I had to do a four-hour presentation for my parents on why I was, at age twenty-three, self sufficient enough to live with a guy who almost positively was my future husband.

Still, James and I somehow were able to create our own world, pulling the best of ourselves to merge together. At work, we were known as Bonnie and Clyde. Either I was number one in sales for the week in the agency, or he was. No one could compete with our energy and desire to push ourselves. James pushed himself to the brink and became our top manager's worst nightmare—the nightmare of being replaced by a rookie. We were young, and after getting just a tiny taste of the big bad world of corporate America, we worked harder than ever to make our dreams a reality. I was able to hold on to my position and make money because as a female, I was not seen as much of a threat to upper management. I was more like eye candy than anything else. My fit frame and wavy long hair, combined with a love of beautiful dresses, made me more of a "girly girl" than a life-insurance closing machine.

"Katerina, don't worry if you don't get the sale," my manager said, seeming compassionate. "Your bonus is still enough for you to go shopping!"

Frustrated by management's inability to take me seriously, I worked tirelessly to prove my ability to close more sales than anyone else. The harder we worked, the harder it was to enjoy life. There simply was no time in the day for going out to eat or dancing at the clubs with our friends. We thought that if we had these big dreams of having nice cars, nice homes, and a nice lifestyle, all the time we put in to achieve those dreams would be worth it—except after we got the nice cars and went on the nice vacation, we found ourselves still plagued with anxiety over the ninety-plus hours a week (including weekends) we were working.

One hot August morning as I was getting ready for work, I realized there was silence coming from the bedroom. I came in the room, thinking I would find James sleeping, but he wasn't. He was lying in bed on his side, staring at the wall.

"What's wrong, James?" I asked him, worried about the state he was in.

"Nothing," he said. He just kept starring at the wall.

"Babe, come on—what's the matter?"

No reply; his eyes didn't even move in my direction. His behavior shocked me, and my heart sank. I couldn't believe I was witnessing one of the top sales reps for our company, a man who was a true go-getter, lying lifeless before my eyes.

I soon learned that he could no longer suppress the knowledge that no matter how hard he worked, no matter how many sales he closed or how big his agency got, there was no chance for him to move up. The system was rigged to catch superstars like him and take away all their business. There was no room for another upper manager—no need for him at all anymore; he was close to being discarded. The system in this particular company was set up so that its agents brought in the clients and trained the new reps. Once they were there for a year and were waiting for their residual income, they were treated in such a way that they had no choice but to quit—and then the residuals would go directly to upper management.

"Fuck it, babe. Just quit!" I told James. "We will figure out a way to pay for everything. You will find another job. You can't let them destroy you." I was trying to bring hope to the situation.

"I can't. If I quit, they'll take all my bonuses and residuals. All my hard work will go to shit," he whispered.

Realizing the magnitude of the situation, even I was out of words of hope. He continued to lie there for days, unable to muster the strength to even to call work to say he wasn't coming in. I watched him fall in to a deep, dark place, where hope wouldn't show its face.

My suggestion was heard but didn't really sink in. James needed something huge to happen, a total shock to our lives in order to create a shift within him … and then it did.

On November 1, 2006, I felt something very different when I woke up. I'd never felt this way before, and I also realized I hadn't had my period in over a month. I took a pregnancy test, and of course our dream of becoming parents was now a reality. We were so excited; we forgot all our troubles and felt a renewed energy within our relationship. I told my parents, and everyone was cautiously happy for us. They said, "Congratulations! How nice," with voices that sounded like they were still trying to process the news.

The next day when I woke up, James was nowhere to be found. I called his cell phone, but he only told me to dress nicely because we were going to PF Chang's in Atlantic City for dinner that night. I thought we were going out to celebrate the baby news, so I didn't question where he was. He came home around five o'clock, smiling nonstop, and I knew there was something he was hiding from me.

"Babe, come here," he said. "Just stand in front of me for a second. I have to ask you something."

Then it dawned on me: he had a box in his hand! *Oh, my God,* I thought. *This is it—the moment I have been dreaming of my entire life and especially since I met James.* I was trying to have fun with him by running away, but he caught me, laid me on the bed, grabbed my face, and kissed me. I melted in his arms, and he helped me up and desperately tried to keep a straight face.

He got on one knee, took my hand, and said, "Marry me, Kat."

My heart was pounding. I'd watched enough movies that I thought a proposal would be a huge event, but it wasn't. It was just us in our bedroom, trying to secure our dreams and our future. I was so excited. I think I said. "All right." We were so happy, and he was so nervous as he put the ring on my right hand. We couldn't stop smiling and laughing—and there were a lot of "oh my Gods" coming out of my mouth.

We got in the car to head out and celebrate in Atlantic City. On our way there, we held hands, and I couldn't help but feel my ring was on the wrong finger.

"Wait, James. Doesn't it go on the left hand?" We burst out laughing.

"I don't know which hand it goes on. I only know which finger it goes on," he said.

I called my parents to tell them the happy news, and of course everyone was so excited for us. "Congratulations. How nice," my mom said, again with a shaky voice, still trying to digest what she'd heard.

It had only been a year since James and I met, and it already felt like this was a long time coming. Truth is, from the moment we met we couldn't wait to get married and start a family. All our thoughts and dreams were of being together for the rest of our lives with all of our children. There was never a talk of a bad time or good time; whenever I got pregnant was when we were becoming parents. Nothing held us back, especially our incredible sex life. The love and passion we had for each other made for mind-blowing lovemaking. I couldn't imagine anyone loving me more deeply than James. I couldn't imagine anyone being in awe of me like he was. We came from two different worlds, but when we were together, we were in our own magnificent world. He always amazed me; he always was thinking of beautiful ways to show me his love.

My favorite place in the world was in his arms. He might not say much, but I could always feel his complete adoration of me. His presence in my life somehow numbed my five senses and super-charged my sixth sense—my heart feeling, my intuition. I didn't need nice gifts or nice words to feel his love. It's funny; we were born just two weeks apart. We used to joke that when we were in heaven, we'd made a pact to come back to earth together and see each other again. Though I was born in Russia, and he was born in America, we, through a series of unusual events, reunited once more!

James and I went to work on a beautiful Tuesday, excited to tell everyone we were pregnant and engaged. I remember walking in, glowing with joy, and suddenly feeling a heavy, negative energy in the office. Our faces, still sore from kissing and smiling, turned stone cold, reflecting the face of our manager.

"Come in, guys. Let's talk," our manager said.

I felt a chill come over my body. We sat in his office, eager to share our happy news. Instead, we heard, "You are both done. I am sorry."

I could feel my heart beating so fast that it gave me a massive headache. *How can we lose our jobs at the same time and just a few days after finding out we are having a baby? How are we going to support ourselves?*

James looked like he was going to cry, but deep down inside I think he was relieved to know he finally could move on to something else. A year of working our asses off well in to the night and on weekends for the hope of one day having enough business on the books that would give us a huge residual income ... and it was for nothing.

We can never get back that time back, but I can't say it was a complete waste of time. We got boot-camp sales training and a work ethic that would prepare us for our future endeavors.

We drove home in silence, doing our best to figure out our next move. Something shifted in us that day because, truthfully, we never were the same again. The downpour of pain, frustration, and a total loss of direction would spiral our lives into a hole so deep and so dark it would take years to fill it with light again. We had no money saved and had to find a place to live. James suggested I move in with my parents, and he would move in with his mom. We packed our cars, taking only what would fit, and drove in two different directions, leaving behind the first house we had made ours, watching it disappear in the rearview mirror.

It was hard moving back into my old bedroom. I felt like such a failure. So many people advised us against moving in together so fast, and the feeling from my parents of "I told you so" left me embarrassed and insecure.

I missed James dearly, and being over an hour apart was more difficult than we thought it would be. A few weeks later, we were able to find real jobs in corporate America. I got a job at a staffing company, and James got a job at a car insurance company. We hated corporate America, and we hated having a salary—getting paid a set amount of money regardless if we were working faster or slower. We'd always worked on commission, and that had fueled our desire for closing more sales. The salaries were so low and the work so mundane that we both fell into deep depression. The deeper we fell into the hole in our minds, the harder it became to communicate and treat each other with love. Arguments became the only way we would express ourselves. During the day, James worked at the insurance company, and at night he worked at the local gas station to make ends meet. How did a college-educated guy who is incredibly gifted in sales end up like that? I felt so bad for him, and he felt even worse for himself.

I was suffering daily with nausea and going to work early in the morning to do work that required attributes I did *not* have. I felt sorry for myself too. I never pictured life this way. I thought we were going to plan a beautiful wedding and then welcome a baby and bring it home to our beautiful townhouse. We were supposed to be cashing ten-thousand-dollar bonuses right around that time, like our managers promised we would on the day they hired us. Everything I thought life would be like, it was not. The more sorry we both felt for ourselves, the further apart we grew. Our fights were fueled by our pain and our resentment toward life, and they were some of the worst arguments we ever had. The cruelty we displayed toward each other would take many years to heal. When things fell apart, I needed to blame someone, even if it was indirectly, because taking responsibility for my life was not something I was mature enough to do.

Finally, around Christmas, after just two months of living apart, James moved in to my parents' house. Things did get better, and after a few nights of holding each other as we fell asleep, we began to heal the wounds of our horrific circumstances. On a really cold day in December, James came home with a massive box from a refrigerator. He asked my dad to help him bring it into the living room, where I was sitting. I just held my head in my hands, wondering what the fuck was going on.

James asked my dad to get the camera; he wanted to show us something. I was growing more and more annoyed with him for ordering my dad around. He finally sat in front of the box, wiping his nose, as it was like a faucet running from the freezing cold winds outside. He handed me a box cutter and said, "Merry Christmas, babe. Open it."

I was so confused as I opened the box. In it was another box from a dishwasher, and in that was another box. I kept opening the boxes to find more boxes. I was drowning in boxes from printers, Christmas lights, and cookies, and finally, I saw a small black box from Macy's. I was in total shock and dismay. I didn't understand why he got me jewelry when we barely had enough money to eat. I opened the box, and the most beautiful, sparkling diamond wedding band emerged.

"I love you, babe," James said. "Let's get married." It was as if he proposed to me all over again, only this time it was as shocking and amazing as I'd always envisioned it to be.

I jumped on him, kissing him and hugging him. "I love you, I love you, I love you so much. Thank you, you crazy son of a gun." My parents hugged us as we jumped up and down with excitement. It was such an amazing moment for us all, and James proved once more how truly deeply he loves me. Truth is, a few days prior I was at Macy's with my friend, trying on wedding bands. I fell in love with that particular band right away, but it was so expensive that I could barely afford to even try it on. While we were at the store, James called me, asking me what I was up to. I told him I'd found my dream wedding band at our local Macy's.

Shortly after we left, he went to that store and asked the sales rep which ring I'd looked at. She showed it to him, and he financed it on the spot. What a great start to a new year. Things were beginning to look up for us. On New Year's Eve, I went out for a walk, thinking about all the amazing and horrific events that had happened that year. I didn't understand the power of visualization and intention, and I focused more on my anxieties for the year, as I was still raw with the emotions of resentment. I was still angry at James and angry that life was not working out the way I envisioned it. I was angry at myself for being too blind to see that we were going to lose our jobs, but we still kept spending as if millions were about to roll in to our accounts.

I was embarrassed to be pregnant and living with my fiancé in my old bedroom. It was against my plan, and just like I judged others for being in the same circumstance, I judged myself with the same animosity. A part of me was very excited and grateful to be pregnant and engaged to someone who wanted so badly to marry me. But most of me was engulfed with negative thoughts, negative emotions, and overall anger for the way my life was. I hated my job, and I hated living with my parents, I hated being poor, and the more I filled my thoughts with hate, the more circumstances I had to hate.

When I went to the doctor for a routine prenatal visit, my test results revealed that I had a very high risk of having a child with Down syndrome. The doctor was shocked to find that I was only twenty-three; I had the test results and risk factors of a forty-two-year-old woman. He suggested we do amniocentesis to determine if the child in fact did have Down syndrome. James and I had to think long and hard about whether we would terminate the pregnancy if we did have a Down syndrome child. We made peace with the decision that we wouldn't keep the baby if it was positive for Down. It was another negative situation to fuel our negative circumstances.

On February 15, 2007, my twenty-fourth birthday, I received a phone call from the doctor's office.

"We got back your test results, and the baby is perfect. Would you like to know the sex?"

I had envisioned being with James on the ultrasound table when we found out, but I thought, *Eh, why not find out over the phone?*

"Yes," I said.

"It's a baby girl."

Oh my goodness! I am going to have a baby girl! I really thought it was a boy, but okay, I'll take it.

James and I were so happy; we decided to name her Juliana. The name came to me because during a rather difficult time in my life, Julia, my dearest cousin, offered me enormous support and love. Anna, my best friend at the time, was also my rock, so honoring her would show my deepest gratitude for all she had done for me. I prayed that Juliana would resemble these extraordinary women I had been so blessed to have in my life.

Eventually, I was fired from my job because I just couldn't force myself to be what I wasn't; I couldn't use skills that hadn't been instilled in me when I was created. I didn't realize it at the time, but God was trying to help me by giving me opportunities that were better suited for the skills I did have. I got a call from an insurance agency that needed someone who was licensed to sell mortgage protection insurance. I took the job right away. I was grateful that I could get back out into the field, make my own schedule, and make money based on my work rather than having a set salary. I again was doing what I did best.

I had a blast meeting with people, and I closed deals nearly every time. I convinced James to leave his gas station and insurance company jobs to come work with me. We finally took back our "Bonnie and Clyde" work persona, crushing it and closing deals daily.

We saved enough money to catch up on bills and began apartment hunting. We found a beautiful one-bedroom apartment with a huge balcony, surrounded by trees, and just twenty minutes away from my parents; it was perfect. A few weeks after moving in, James insisted that we get married before the baby arrived.

My brother suggested Tavern on the Green for our wedding

celebration, and by some miracle, they offered a wonderful menu in our price range. We got married on May 4 in the New Brunswick City Hall and had our celebration on May 5.

It was a perfect spring day, and all those dearest to our hearts were in attendance. It was one of the happiest days of our lives. The room where we held our celebration had glass walls and was completely filled with sunlight. So much love was in that room, and we were so grateful for the beautiful words everyone offered us. At one point, James wrapped his arms around me, and as I rested my head on his chest, I could feel his heart pounding. His soft lips pressed against my forehead. This was my man, and there was no one in the world I would rather have been with than him. The day was magical, and after the lunch was finished, we took a ride on the horse carriage around Central Park. God had one more gift for me: as we galloped through a quaint section of the park, a few musicians played Vivaldi's "Spring" for us. It is my favorite composition, and I listened to it almost daily for many years. It was the first time in a very long time that I felt like God was on my side, offering me a truce for all the misfortune we had been through.

Just two weeks later, I had the most beautiful baby shower I ever could have imagined. Friends and family gathered to show me their love and support and to shower me with gifts. It was the first time I wasn't embarrassed to be pregnant. I was married and living in my own apartment. I was right on track with the vision I had for my life. Although life was good, however, it wasn't great. I still had not yet mastered the art of living without anxious thoughts and worry dominating my mind. I feared losing control of my life again, and I figured that worrying about losing control was the best way to prevent losing control. I did the best I could, but all that changed eight weeks later.

On June 23 I woke up feeling unusually energized and craved a long walk on the boardwalk by the ocean. I called my mom, and she agreed to meet me. As I walked, I felt my water break but not in the traditional water leaking; it was more of a slow trickle, and I got very anxious. I drove back home and told my doctor I was coming to the hospital. I was so excited and nervous about finally meeting my baby girl. I took a long shower, and I just broke down in tears. I was very scared of labor; I didn't know what to expect. Even though I'd read so many books on the process of labor and birth, no amount of information can prepare one for such a major event.

We arrived at the hospital, and the doctor said I had not yet dilated, but they would give me some drugs to get my body moving faster. Since my water slightly broke, the doctor decided to break my water fully, again in hope that it would speed things up a bit. It was around 6:00 p.m. when I checked in, and I spent the night sleeping, waiting for the contractions to start. By six o'clock the following morning, nothing was happening. My body refused to go in to labor, even though my water had broken almost twelve hours before. I was tense, scared, and completely lost in my own negative thinking. I wasn't allowed to get up and walk around, as I was strapped to the bed with monitors on my belly. The doctor ordered Pitocin to force my body into labor, and it did.

I finally began to feel steady contractions, but unfortunately, I was not progressing. The doctor increased my dose to the maximum amount. The pain was so excruciating that I begged for an epidural. I know James and my mom were in the room with me the entire time, but I couldn't see or hear anything. My body was exhausted from all the drugs I was given, and when the epidural was finally administered I began to shake to the point of vomiting. *This is horrible*, I thought. *This is not the way I envisioned giving birth. I can't even think straight. My body hurts so badly, even after the epidural.*

After hours and hours of contractions, I was still stuck at five centimeters. The doctor said he could no longer keep drugging me and that a C-section was the only way to get the baby out. I was crushed, and felt broken and like my body had failed me.

On June 24, 2007, at 7:30 p.m., as I lay on the operating table, I heard the most beautiful sound in the world—my baby girl cried for the first time. James and I were so relieved and happy to finally meet our first child. The nurse brought her to me, and I nuzzled her warm, delicious-smelling, perfect face. It was at that exact moment that I understood real happiness, real love, and such a sense of purpose. I was so in awe of the experience that I quickly forgot the long, painful journey that brought me to this moment. When I held my magnificent gift from God, I looked into her eyes, and it was as if her soul and mine were intertwined.

Her presence and energy was the spark I so badly needed to set my entire being on fire and burning with love so deep that it erased any pain I ever felt.

There was something almost magical about her—I could see God's light in her, and I was mesmerized by her beauty. The most beautiful girl in the world was in my arms, to love, to hold, to raise, and to be with through eternity.

Interestingly, number seven is the number of God. Her name, Juliana, has seven letters, and she was born in the seventh hour, seven days before the seventh month in the year 2007. She was godly to me. I felt God's presence—probably for the first time in life—when I was near her.

Our time together was the most magical time of my life. She brought out in me such a strong maternal instinct that I never questioned my choices of what I needed to do for her. She loved being in my arms and sleeping on my chest, and my heart flooded with love with each beat. Before she was born, I had decided I would put her in the bassinet to sleep and feed her formula. I was positive that this kid wasn't going to change our lifestyle and that she would be the most independent baby anyone ever knew. I sneered at my friends who slept with their kids. How could they give up their bed (and the sex) to share it with a baby? How could they allow their babies to wrap the parents around their fingers? *Sorry, not me,* I thought. *I run this house, not the baby!*

I came home from the hospital, however, with zero memory of having those thoughts. Juliana was my whole world, and I was at her service, ready to do anything to make her happy and make her smile. I selflessly poured my heart into her.

Not a night was spent apart, not a moment without each other. I even took her to work with me every day, never giving a thought to being anywhere she wasn't. Of course, this put a strain on my relationship with James. While I was basking in the bliss of motherhood, he missed being the better part of my life. Often he would ask me to drop off the baby at my parents' house so we could go out, but the thought of it set off anxiety attacks within me that I just couldn't deal with.

The closer Juliana and I grew, the further James and I drifted apart. It took a lot of convincing for me to finally go out to lunch with him a few weeks after she was born. As we enjoyed our sushi, however, I was counting the seconds before I could be with her again. I felt so good with her—there was no discussion of money or lack thereof. She didn't have mood swings, and we didn't discuss serious matters that ignited panic or worry within me. I wanted to be with her, and there were no problems to deal with, just blissful joy. With her, I would step out of my real world and into a heavenly place. With James, I would step out of my heavenly place into a hellish world, where anxiety, arguments, and financial woes prevailed. Juliana was my escape.

Chapter 2

When Juliana was about four weeks old, James lost his job. All the child-care, home-care, and financial responsibilities now lay heavily on my shoulders. I felt as if I was doing it all, when all I wanted was to be home with Juliana, not on appointments with clients. I wanted to snuggle with her, not cradle the car seat with my foot as I made my sales presentations. The strain on my marriage began to gain weight, but I didn't address the issues; I just went deeper in to the world I shared with Juliana, suppressing all my relationship problems. I hid within her embrace, ignoring everything else around me. Her presence in my life was such a gift; she healed me with every breath she took. I spent many nights holding her, praying for her, and thanking God for bestowing this privilege upon me. *What have I done in my life to deserve such joy,* I thought, *such blissful, deep love?*

As she got a little older and days of snuggling turned to weeks and then months, she began to change. I began to feel like she was taking care of me, not the other way around. One night when she was about four months old, I lay next to her, nursing her to sleep. She looked up at me, her eyes twinkling in the dark, and with her soft hand she caressed my cheek in the most gentle way. I could feel her love for me engulfing my entire body and soul. I closed my eyes and held on to the warmth of her hand and the euphoria I was feeling. It was the highest feeling a human being is capable of; it is the reason we are given children—to awaken emotions that were bottled for many years. My sweet baby girl caressed me to sleep that way every night, giving me all her love and thanking me for the way I loved her, cared for her, and made her feel. I couldn't get enough of her and was always ready to serve her and do anything for her.

Some well-meaning friends and family told me that I held her too much or that I gave her way too much attention; they warned me that she would get "spoiled." I never understood how the term "spoiled" could relate to a child. I always thought that term was for food in the fridge that was ignored and then spoiled. How could I shower my little baby with affection and love, only to have her spoil? The definition didn't make sense to me. You can't spoil babies; they are meant to be adored. Leaving them in their cribs to cry, like you leave leftovers in the fridge to rot, is spoiling, but tending to their every need is a natural act of a mother who is one with her child. It was my constant attachment to her that helped my body produce an abundant milk supply. We were so close; she drew out my maternal instinct. I never heard her cry; she was always happy, no matter what she was feeling.

During the day we spent many hours playing and going for long walks. In the evening we would get dressed and head to work. When James finally got a day job and didn't have to work evenings in the insurance company for which I was working, he would stay and play with her. My brother, Max, was also a huge part of our lives, especially as Juliana got older and wasn't happy sitting in a car seat for long periods of time. He would come over to babysit her as often as he could. He was all about music and couldn't live without it. On the evenings he was with her, I could hear the music blasting as I came near our apartment building. I would walk in to find him holding her as they danced together, laughing and singing!

Sometimes during our nightly embrace, I felt anxiety I just couldn't shake off. I had visions—or rather, an intuitive feeling—where I saw James cleaning out the refrigerator and throwing out the numerous bags of frozen breast milk. I saw him go into my closet and take down all of Juliana's clothing. I had a recurring thought of her dying and not being with me forever. It was so real to me that I began to tell her she would always be my baby because I couldn't see a future with her; I just couldn't picture her walking or talking. The closer we got, the more I began to sense something was wrong. Her smile seemed to mask her pain. At night, she caressed me to sleep; she almost never fell asleep first. She began to no longer seem like a baby to me but more like a guardian angel. I was at her service, but she was serving me with enormous doses of love and appreciation every single day. Her rosy cheeks began to fade, and her face got more pale, almost blue, with each day. I took her to the doctor a few times, but no one could find anything wrong. The doctor blamed her pale face on December's lack of sunlight.

We celebrated Christmas at our home, but I felt like a storm was coming. Something big was going to happen, and I felt that I had to conserve all my energy for whatever it was. The more anxiety I felt and the more I was overwhelmed with fear, the more Juliana attempted to nourish me with her love. She began to morph into something that wasn't a baby but a full-grown massive light. Miracles were happening every day; I was able to communicate with her through my heart. I would feel anxious that something would happen to her, and she would reach for me, caressing my face, attempting to calm me, or she'd smile at me from across the room.

I remember learning in yeshiva when I was in the fourth grade that before babies are born, they are told everything that will happen to them. Then an angel touches their upper lips, leaving a dip so that they will not be able to speak of what they know. As they get older, they begin to forget what their angel told them, and by the time they can speak, their memory of all they know is long gone.

One day, Juliana woke up from a nap, and her neck seemed tense; it forced her head to lean to the left. I assumed it was because she had slept in a weird position, so I didn't give it much thought. Days went by, and she woke up every day, vomiting not spitting up. I took her to the doctor, who agreed that Juliana's sore neck was from sleeping in the wrong position and possibly that she had a stomach virus.

Shortly after she turned seven months and a few weeks of having this neck pain, her symptoms began to manifest more visibly. Besides the vomiting, the left side of her face began to swell, looking like she had a minor stroke. I was in denial and petrified of what this might be. I was at a loss of what to do.

On January 30, we held James's twenty-fifth birthday celebration at our house. My brother and parents joined us in toasting him and showering him with gifts. While we all smiled, we knew something was wrong with Juliana. She wasn't happy; we could see it in her eyes, which looked sickly and in pain. Her left side was now visibly more swollen; her pale face had a greenish cast. She tried to smile through the pain, but we all saw the twinkle in her eyes disappearing. I was scared to take her to the doctor—scared to find out what was wrong.

When my mother suggested I take her to the hospital I yelled at her, "Stop telling me what to do! She's fine!" I began to cry and held Juliana close to me, whispering, "She's fine; she's fine."

After everyone left, I lay down with her, and as I held her, I knew she wasn't okay. Her left arm and leg began to shake, and she barely mustered up the strength to reach for my face like she always did. I felt like I was in her arms, like I was desperately trying to stay in my happy place within her love, her warmth, and her amazing energy. A feeling came over me that this might be our last night together. Fighting that overwhelmingly fearful thought, I fell asleep in her embrace, holding on to her and to my happy place, my escape from reality.

The next morning I woke up in a puddle of vomit. As if a higher being took over me, I got up and got dressed. I had only one place in mind: the hospital. After nursing her all night, her diaper was dry. I knew that this day was the last day I could hold off on taking her to the hospital, and I was petrified. I dressed her in her pink teddy-bear overalls, my favorite look for her, though they did little to decorate her crying, swollen face. I didn't tell anyone where I was going. All I could think of was getting an answer to the question that had been burning a hole inside me: *what is wrong with my baby girl?*

On the way to the hospital, everything looked different to me—the sky was dark, and the once-beautiful trees looked lifeless. We arrived at the hospital around noon and were welcomed by a wonderful nurse, whose warmth felt so calming. Within a few minutes we were escorted to a waiting room. A doctor came in and looked at Juliana with his flashlight, making her laugh as he shined the light in her eyes.

"I am going to need a CAT scan immediately," he said to the nurse.

I didn't think anything of it. I thought it was protocol for all children who vomited. The nurse gave Juliana a mild sedative and asked me to hold her until she fell asleep. As she lay nursing in my arms, she looked comfortable as she drifted off to sleep. I put her in the crib that would be wheeled in to the CAT scan room. I called James to tell him we were at the hospital and that he should come over right away. Luckily, his office was a few minutes away, and he arrived shortly before she was wheeled back into the room. We had a few moments to talk and tried to lighten up the dreary mood that permeated the room. Juliana was still groggy from the medicine but somehow was able to smile when she saw her daddy.

"Hey, buddy, how are you feeling?" James said with a huge smile and in a high-pitched voice.

She tried to sit up but threw up all over herself. Her eyes were sickly and watery, and she raised her hands, wanting me to hold her. As I picked her up, she felt so weak it was like holding dead weight. I kept kissing her head as I whispered, "I love you so much, my love. I love you. You're going to be okay."

Just as I was enjoying our embrace, I heard the sound of the metal curtain clips slide across the metal beams in the ceiling. The sudden noise startled me. I turned around and saw a short bald man with glasses, wearing white scrubs and clutching to a clipboard. His face was still and his eyes sympathetic. James smiled and extended his hand, saying, "I'm James, and this is my wife, Katerina. How are ya?"

"My name is Dr. Kohn. I want to talk to you about your daughter," he said as he shook James's hand. I picked up Juliana in my arms and made funny faces at her, hoping to make her smile. As our faces were locked on each other, I heard the doctor say, "Your daughter has a large brain tumor; it's on her brain stem."

"Will she die?" These were the only words I was able to blurt out.

"I can't say," he said sympathetically.

Suddenly, my heart dropped. I felt dizzy and nauseated. It felt exactly like a dream you pray to God to wake up from. It was surreal, yet absolutely devastating. I felt my whole body shake. I felt paralyzed, unable to speak or move. I looked at Juliana, and it all came together.

I kept muttering, "No, no, no," but on the inside I was screaming, *No, no, no! Please, God, no!*

Every cell of my body was praying for this to be a nightmare, but it wasn't. As the minutes passed, and Juliana kept vomiting, I knew deep inside that to ask if she would live would only destroy me more. I asked the nurse to keep an eye on Juliana, and I went outside to smoke a cigarette. I sat there on the edge of the sidewalk, smoking cigarette after cigarette, trying desperately to wake up from this nightmare. The whole time I was outside, I didn't realize that James was right behind me on the bench, speechless, devastated, and petrified of the battle ahead. We sat in silence, apart from each other.

As I stood up to walk back in, James grabbed my hand and said, "Listen, no matter what happens, we have each other. Let's live off that. It's the only way I'll survive."

Holding hands, we went back into the hospital. The doctor said he must operate as soon as possible to alleviate the pressure in her heard and to slow the vomiting. The date for surgery was set for February 4, 2008, just three days after her diagnosis. Two, four, eight—all even numbers. I grasped on to the idea that it might bring us luck. At that moment, I grasped on to anything that would alleviate the horror I was feeling. The nurses helped us to our room on the Pediatric ICU floor—the floor of nightmares; the floor where parents walk around like zombies; the floor where tears and prayers dominate the faces of loved ones; the floor you never want to visit, let alone call home.

The room had a crib as well as a cot for me sleep on. I told the nurses, "My daughter will not sleep alone or without me." I somehow convinced them to bring in a bed so that I could hold my very sick daughter through the night. As I lay near my sweet baby girl, I was weak but so angry. I was consumed with one thought: *why?* Why was this happening? And what was God's plan for me, for us, for Juliana?

No matter how terrible the situation seemed, I always had a feeling in my heart that it was all happening for a reason. I had faith in God, not because I was religious but because of a tugging feeling in my heart that made me feel like a higher power had a plan for us. I just trusted my intuition that this was part of a master plan, happening in divine order.

I fell asleep with my lips on Juliana's head, praying for her, attempting to heal her with my love. I didn't really sleep; all I could do was lie still in silence. I asked James to go home and bring back our favorite funny movies so that we could laugh and raise the energy of the room—anything to get our minds off the horror that was our life. At that moment, I decided we weren't going to succumb to sadness. We would succumb to laughter and find the strength to smile for our sad, sick daughter. I held her on my chest, near my breasts, nursing her nonstop the entire weekend.

Monday was the day of her surgery, and after five in the morning, I was not allowed to nurse her anymore because she would be under anesthesia. I didn't care. She looked at me and pulled at my shirt, begging for my milk. I let her nurse anyway. It was the last time she would do so.

The doctors came in and escorted us to the surgery room. I was able to carry her there in my arms. As I held her, I couldn't stop kissing her and telling her I loved her. I sang her favorite lullabies, and it seemed to calm her. The surgeon came in and held out his arms for me to give her to him. He picked her up, and she began to cry. Not a painful cry but a sad cry. As he walked away with her, she was on his shoulder, looking at me with tearful eyes. To this day it is the most painful, most replayed moment of my life. It was the last time I would hold her; the last time I would see her crying face; the, last time I would see her eyes.

She never woke up from the surgery, but she was still alive, her soul fighting to stay in her sick body. The next six hours were spent with family—in agony, in prayer, in hope.

Finally, the doctors came out to the waiting room. One said, "The tumor is very large and is attached to her brain stem. It's one of the rarest, deadliest cancerous tumors in nature, called an atypical teratoid rhabdoid tumor. She has a 10 percent chance of surviving the first year. Treatment will be aggressive."

I felt my heart sinking, and I could feel my body go numb. After that, I felt nothing. I walked out of the hospital to meet my mom, and we ran toward each other, unable to wait another second for the comforting embrace of one another. I didn't need to tell her anything; she knew. As we held each other, all my emotions were reignited, and I broke down in tears, sobbing uncontrollably. I buried my head in her neck and wept until I couldn't breathe anymore.

I never lose control of my emotions. I always find a reason to wipe my tears and prepare for battle. I don't like it when people see me looking weak, even if it's my mother. I didn't want to break her heart; I know the pain a mother feels when her child is suffering. I felt so helpless, and at that moment, I decided I was going to be strong for my daughter, for the whole family. I felt guilty for feeling pain. Juliana was the one experiencing this horrible disease and was about to go through the battle of her life, not me. I took a deep breath, closed my eyes, and begged for all the strength in world to come to me—as you would brace yourself before going on a very scary roller coaster. I smiled on the outside but was petrified on the inside. I had no idea what lay before me.

I walked in to our hospital room and watched the nurses wheel our baby girl into the room. She lay silent and still, and I could see that life had left her beautiful face. She was alive only with the help of a ventilator. She survived the twelve-hour extremely intense surgery, but the meaning of "alive" was that she had a heartbeat—that was all.

The next few days were filled with hope and hopelessness. Laughter and tears. Strength and debilitating weakness. A neurologist from Egypt came in to check on Juliana. He was older and seemed wiser than everyone else, and I felt the withering of a soul whose life career has worn out his compassion and hope.

He sat on the bed next to me and said, "After forty years of seeing cases like this, all I can recommend to you is to take her home. Let her die at home. Treatment has a very small chance of working but a high chance of being painful."

I was so mad at him. How dare he tell me this? How dare he tell me the truth? How dare he suggest such a course of action? We would fight until the end. What if she was a rare case? What if she lived? How could I have brought in a happy child, and now, just three days later, be asked to take her home to let her die?

On the morning of February 14, James snuck into the hospital room at six o'clock, before going to work, and placed a Valentine's Day card by my bedside. It was such a happy, much-needed moment for me. I didn't feel like I was alone, and for a short moment I felt blessed, grateful, and in love. It was also on this day that I had no choice but to quit my job because I knew I wasn't returning any time soon. Luckily, James was still employed and the insurance with his company was excellent. We were safe—for now.

On February 15, 2008, my twenty-fifth birthday, we were moved to Hackensack Medical Center, a facility that was better able to administer protocol for such a rare tumor. Only thirty-five kids worldwide have been reported to have this kind of tumor. It was so rare and so unusual for such a young baby that the woman who discovered this tumor in 1988 came out of retirement to inspect the biopsy results, ultimately concluding that it was, in fact, the deadly tumor ATRT. As I packed our bags prior to leaving, the driver of the ambulance who would transport Juliana spoke to me for a little bit. He seemed compassionate, and he radiated so much love that it was healing and reassuring to me that we were going to the right place.

The drive across the New Jersey Turnpike felt long. The sun was shining, but I felt a dark cloud above my head and in my heart. I was thinking about what the last few weeks had been like, and I wondered how I was going to recover from this. I thought about the day being my birthday—I'd never thought I would be spending this special day in moving my sweet baby girl between hospitals. I felt betrayed by God, by life, and by fate. But then I realized that it was not about me. I wasn't the one diagnosed with this rare tumor. I wasn't about to do ten rounds of chemo. I was not bedridden. I was not hanging on to life. My beautiful Juliana was, and for her, I could easily forget about me.

It's easier to live for other people, to be strong for them, to support them. The hard part is dealing with ourselves. I had to be a source of strength, positive energy, love, and hope. I put on the mask of a superhuman, not realizing the repercussions of this decision. It would haunt me very long into the future.

Hackensack Medical is a hotel-style hospital, with all the amenities of a five-star resort. Our room was huge and had bright orange walls, the exact color of our bedroom at home. Shortly after I settled in, the ambulance driver wheeled my beauty into the room. After the nurses disconnected the portable breathing machine and connected the ventilator, we were left alone. The only sound in the room was the ventilator, breathing for my baby girl. I lay next to her, nuzzling my nose against her silky soft cheeks. I inhaled her sweet smell. I sang her our favorite song, and I whispered in her ear, "I'm here. I'm here. I'm always going to be here." It was my birthday, and amid the horror I felt lucky to be spending my first birthday as a mother—my yearly birthday wish since I was a little girl.

It was a long drive to Hackensack Medical, so my parents,

brother, and James were coming the next day, Saturday. At eleven o'clock on the night of my birthday, however, my then best friend, Anna, came with bags of Chinese food and two bottles of champagne. I was so happy. I felt so much love for her. She was the only person who could make me laugh until I peed, and I needed her desperately. We convinced the security guard to open the cafeteria so that we had a place to eat and drink, but he couldn't turn on the lights since we weren't supposed to be there. The cafeteria had an enormous fish tank that illuminated the area with a beautiful blue light. We talked, laughed, ate, and drank, celebrating my birthday under this magnificent light. It was such a source of energy and strength for me. I felt so blessed. I felt my friend's love, and I felt God's warmth attempting to answer the prayers of all those who loved me.

Days went by, and Juliana's health deteriorated. She suffered two massive strokes, lost her hearing, became cross-eyed, and had a shunt in her brain that wouldn't work no matter what the doctors tried. She underwent three rounds of very intense chemotherapy, and I spent many nights by her side, wiping the vomit off her face. All I could do was hold and kiss her hand and beg God to have mercy on her. I asked the head doctor why we hadn't see any signs that she was ill. How could such a happy baby be in so much pain, and we saw nothing of it?

He said, "Because you breast-fed her. She was healthy, and she also got painkillers from your milk. You should be very proud that you chose to nurse her on demand. That is what kept her pain down."

At that moment I realized something so important about maternal instinct. I hadn't listened to the people who said I shouldn't worry so much about breast-feeding because formula was a great option too. I was so happy I hadn't listened to anyone who said to let her "cry it out," and she would learn to fall asleep on her own, I held her every night, making sure she was always happy, because that's what felt right to me. I followed my instinct to mother her with love and compassion and to satisfy her every need. The choices I'd made eliminated my guilt; I knew I'd done everything to give her the best life possible. I poured my heart and soul—my everything—into this child, the gift God gave me.

One night Juliana was tired of breathing, and her chest began to cave in. The nurse called a Code Red, and many doctors ran in, trying to save her. They performed CPR and ultimately intubated her. I watched in horror as my eight-month-old baby, who now weighed only twelve pounds, fought for her life, I stepped out of the room to gather myself.

As I stepped into the hallway and glanced toward the room next door, I couldn't believe my eyes. A boy was dying. His father was removing the tube from his mouth and was nervously waiting for his son's heart to stop. The monitors on the Pediatric ICU were outside of the rooms. As I watched his heart rate slow, I also saw that all the monitors of the other children displayed very fast heart rates and breathing rates. When the boy's heart finally flat-lined, within seconds all the vitals of all the kids on the floor went back to normal. I was speechless. *These children are all connected,* I thought. *They are all hovering above their bodies as we try to save their lives. They all love each other and feel for each other. They are all angels, waiting for their time to finally be free from their disease-ridden bodies.*

That was the first time I realized how connected we humans are when we don't put up walls. We have such love for each other when we put our guards down. It was also the moment I realized that if Juliana became one of the angels, her soul would be so much happier. Children are not meant to be bedridden, blind, deaf, or awakened in the middle of the night because a breathing tube needs to be readjusted. The thought of her dying was no longer a fear; it was actually comforting. I would rather deal with the pain of losing her than watch her suffer as she fought for her life because I wanted her to live, to be with me. At that moment I let go of the fear that paralyzed me—the fear that made me sick to my stomach and haunted my thoughts. I accepted her fate. If she was to die, then I would not fight it. I told the doctors to put a Do Not Resuscitate order on her file. Suddenly, I felt light; I felt no pain. I felt her love pour in to me. I felt her spirit, and I knew that she was no longer in her body but hovering, waiting to break free from the tubes, the monitors, and the pain.

I stood close to her, and with tears in my eyes I whispered in her ear, "If you're done fighting and want to be free, then go. I will be fine. I love you no matter what happens, no matter where you are. You are always in one place—in my heart. Be free. Be happy. I love you."

I asked one the of nurses to place her in my arms. I needed to hold her, to feel her, to comfort her. The nurse disconnected all the machinery and only left a breathing tube in. Finally, after weeks of fearing to pick her up because it might hurt her, I was free to do what I desired. As she lay in my arms, I rubbed my lips against her soft hair as I always did when we would fall asleep together. It was so calming. I feel asleep, and so did she. We both had the sweetest sleep we'd had in weeks.

Her vitals were perfect—her heart rate was amazingly calm, and her blood pressure was at its lowest in days. She was happy. She felt my love, and we were in heaven together. The sound of the door opening and nurses talking startled me, waking me from my blissful sleep. At first, I forgot where I was, but then the deep, dark reality of what was happening settled in. My peaceful smile faded from my lips, and my eyes began to fill with tears, as they had for the past few weeks. Shortly after, a doctor walked in and needed to send Juliana for an MRI. He startled us, and her heart rate and blood pressure skyrocketed. He said he needed to get the test done at 5:00 a.m. He rudely told me he had a job to do.

Juliana's vitals never recovered. Two days later, on March 15, as I lay next to her, she began to bleed from all her incisions. Her body was breaking down. I gave her a sponge bath, washing her slowly with warm water and delicious-smelling baby wash. I knew the end was near. I felt her deeper and deeper within me, which meant to me that she was beginning her descent from her body. I whispered in her ear over and over again, "Be free. I love you."

The next morning, March 16, James asked me to have lunch with him alone, outside of the hospital. The previous six weeks had been very hard on us. I was living full time at Juliana's bedside, and he was working full time, trying desperately to preserve whatever we had left at home. I was unable to work, and so James was our only source of income. The stress of everything, the lack of having a life together, and the inability to cope with such heartache almost destroyed us.

My brother came to pick me up around eleven that morning. I kissed Juliana good-bye and promised I would be back soon. As I was leaving, I noticed that her pointer finger had a small cut on it, and it was pointing upward. She got my attention not because her finger was pointing up—the stroke made her hands do weird things—but because it was cut. As my brother and I left, I had a feeling something was going to happen. One of the nurses told me that when children die, they usually wait for their parents to leave the room; that thought stayed with me. As we were driving to East Brunswick to meet James, I was looking at the sky, trying to find God or hope or beauty, trying to find a reason to smile. All I saw was darkness—he depth of hell on earth.

We went to Shogun 27 for a hibachi meal. We couldn't bear to look at each other, so we needed a distraction. As the chef served us our food, I got a phone call from the hospital.

"You need to come back as soon as possible," the nurse said. "Juliana is no longer responsive."

As if in slow motion, I looked at James, looked at the food, and almost threw up from the nervousness. He understood it was time to leave.

The drive to the hospital was about an hour, but it felt like an eternity to us both. I prayed the entire time. I called on all my deceased family members to help me. I called every single power on earth to give me strength. James pulled up to the hospital entrance.

I jumped from the car, ran through the front door, and headed for the stairs—I couldn't wait for the elevator. As I ran up the stairs, skipping steps to get to Juliana faster, I finally got to the fourth floor, completely out of breath. I pushed open the door on the floor, and as I ran down the hall, I could see Juliana's corner room. As I got closer to her room, I saw what was happening. Two doctors stood over her. One doctor was jamming a massive needle in her head—this was a test they did to determine if someone was brain dead—but she was completely unresponsive. My heart was pounding from running but more so because I knew that this was my baby's last day on earth. I felt the battle for life end. It was the last time I would run down these halls in a frantic panic, as I had many times before this day. I took a deep breath and braced myself.

I walked in and saw her face. My body felt so light, and I felt joy for a few seconds. She was so peaceful. She was no longer in pain. There was no straining to fight for life. She looked like an angel. All the strength for which I'd prayed came to me, and I felt it in every cell of my body. I felt relief; it was such a pleasure to see her so peaceful, and I accepted her death. I finally understood the beauty of death, I finally understood that the pain I'd felt was solely because she was in pain. We were so connected; I felt everything she felt. Now that she felt no pain, I too felt no pain.

James had parked the car, and when he joined me in the room, I didn't have to say anything. The shunt that was pumping brain fluid through her head was full of blood. He saw no life in her, just a monitor that displayed her heart rate, which was beginning to slow down. I hugged him, burying my head in his chest. "Our baby ... our beautiful baby girl ..."

We called our parents, and everyone came to say their good-byes. We were going to take her off life support and wanted everyone she loved and who loved her to be there. Once everyone arrived, each person had a few minutes to say good-bye. When it was my turn, I leaned in close to her and took a deep breath, as if to savior the sweetness of her smell, as only a mother can appreciate.

I whispered in her ear, "My sweet love, thank you for choosing me to be your mother. You have brought so much joy into my life, so much love. I am forever grateful for all you showed me. Please bless me with more children. Please look after me, look after your siblings, and look after all of us. Never leave my side, I will always look for you, and I will always feel you. I love you so much. I will miss you, but I will see you again when my time comes."

I stayed close to her, holding and kissing her hands, and finally I kissed her forehead, the way a mother does when it's time to say good night. I left the room, and James was left alone with her. He was going to pull out her breathing tube and hold her until her heart stopped and her soul left her body. I couldn't bear to witness her dying; I didn't care what anyone thought of my decision. Juliana's heat began to beat when we were together, and it would cease to beat when she was with her father.

I was in another room, with my head in my hands, praying for God to open up the gates of heaven and receive this beautiful angel. I prayed for her to drift off into the atmosphere to be one with God, to be free, and to be where she was supposed to be—in a place where pain didn't exist and only love dominated the existence. I felt that she was too good for this earth. Her time here was short and mostly very happy. I felt relief; the war was over. The fight was over. I now could go on to live the life I was meant to live out there in the world, having more children and enjoying daily blessings, not in a hospital room by my baby's bedside, drowning in agony, hopelessness, and pain. I was meant to watch my children grow and thrive, not deteriorate and die a little bit every day. I felt her light inside me, and I almost felt guilty to be so relieved.

The doctor walked in and said she had passed away. I walked back in the room, and I watched James hold her lifeless body. He was crying and kissing her, trying to savor every last moment with her. He gave her to me. I hadn't held her in my arms without all the machines connected to her, not even a breathing tube, since the morning of her surgery; it had been six weeks. She was still warm. I was surprised how much she had grown; she was so much taller. It felt so good to hold her. I kissed her again and said, "Thank you. I love you." I put her down in the bed, and we left the room.

Our parents hugged us and hugged each other, and we all made a promise to get through this together. I believe Juliana was smiling. She loved it when everyone was together and happy.

In the elevator on our way down, we met anther family who had just lost their son to cancer as well. "How long was your battle?" I asked.

The father looked at me with red, teary eyes. "Ten years," he said.

My heart sank, and I suddenly felt like the luckier one in this elevator that was filled with heartbroken people, who, just minutes ago, had lost their children. This man's answer got me through the next few days. Instead of crying out of despair and feeling like God had forsaken me, I felt lucky that our little precious angel only suffered a mere six weeks. In retrospect, I see that while it was happening, it seemed like decades, but we, as a family, suffered for such a short time.

James and I held hands on our drive home from the hospital.

"We will never have another problem again," I said. "We learned the concept of problems at age twenty-five."

James squeezed my hand in agreement. We came home to the place where we had all our memories of Juliana—where I'd brought her home for the first time, where she learned how to sit up and roll over. James was kind enough to put away all of her clothing and toys and anything that would remind me of her.

As God would have it, our lease was up the very next morning, and we were moving back into my old bedroom at my parents' house.

I lay in bed, the bed where I'd spent countless hours snuggling, playing with, inhaling, and singing to my dearest baby. The bed that was vibrating so much love, but it was now the only place on earth I didn't want to be. I couldn't sleep, as the events of the last few days played in my head, over and over again.

I couldn't believe what had happened. I would spend my lifetime figuring out what the purpose of this was and what I would do with this experience. I thought about how different my life would be now. Before, I was plagued with anxiety, always living in fear of losing those I loved. I couldn't fully enjoy life. I didn't understand life; to understand it, I had to see death. It's hard to enjoy the little things in life, the little blessings we get all day long, without fully experiencing the nightmare that life can be. It puts everything in perspective.

I always thought that cancer and sickness was sort of a gift from God. It gave us the understanding that time was running out and that it was imperative to express love and appreciation for the person who would soon be leaving this earth. I know many people who lost their loved ones in accidents and who spent their lives in regret because they didn't get a chance to fix their relationships or say "I love you" one last time. That night, I felt like I got a second chance, and I felt a very strong urge to live out my life the way Juliana would have wanted me to. This was not only Juliana's last night on earth but my last night in the home that was built on joyful memories.

The next morning, James and I moved back home with my parents, back into my old bedroom. It was a wonderful move. I was back where I'd started, and it felt like a clean slate. I had to rebuild my life from scratch. I went from having my own apartment, my own little family, and a great-paying (and satisfying) job to having just my closest family. That was a great foundation to begin with.

The funeral was held on March 21, the day after my sister-in-law gave birth to her first son. Our family experienced death and birth, hours apart. It was a bittersweet time; we rejoiced the birth of a new family member while our hearts were still aching with the pain of losing Juliana. God has an interesting way of doing things.

As we arrived at the funeral home in New Brunswick, I felt the numbness melt away and was overwhelmed with enormous sorrow. I was alone in the room, looking at this tiny casket covered with hundreds of flowers, and all I could do was put my head down and think about our journey together, from the moment I held Juliana for the first time and cried with joy to the moment I held her for the last time and cried with sorrow. I thought about how much I learned from her—how fragile life is; that you don't have time to waste, regardless of how old you are. Life can change its course within seconds. I thought about how grateful I was that I'd had a guiding power whispering in my ear, telling me to fully enjoy her and give her the best life possible. Some people live to be seventy and rarely experience the bliss she had in a mere seven months before she got sick.

I felt pain. I felt like I was in a dream, but I also felt relief in knowing she was no longer in pain. I could deal with my own pain, but watching her suffer was more painful than I could bear. Comforting her just wasn't enough.

As people began to flood the room, I felt so much love and compassion from everyone. They came from everywhere—people who didn't know us but had heard about our story; people from my childhood whom I hadn't seen in over a decade. James's entire fraternity came to show support and love. We received flowers from all over the country, so many that we almost ran out of space. I know Juliana was smiling to see so much support and love offered to her family that she loved so much. I felt her near me. I felt her inside me, and I felt her comforting me.

I couldn't even cry. When I stood up to give the eulogy, I asked everyone to use this tragedy as a wake-up call to love more, hug more, and forgive more and to not let her life end in vain. I truly believe life doesn't give us difficult situations to punish us but to awaken us, to give my daughter's life a purpose, I had to spread what she stood and died for, which was life—to feel alive, to feel awake, to feel love, to feel joy. To be alive is not just a heart beating in a soulless, motionless body. It's so much more. In retrospect, I see that I only understood these lessons in my head; understanding them in my heart took many more years.

We decided to cremate Juliana and put her ashes in the ocean at one of the most beautiful locations I have ever been to. In Long

35

Beach Island, New Jersey, there is a playground where James played throughout his entire childhood. There is a bench overlooking the bay, and the water is always still, and the sunsets leave a path of sparkles. It almost looks like the path to heaven, lit up like magic. We put her ashes there so that she would be one with water, dancing in it and enjoying her freedom. She didn't belong underground. I always feel peaceful by bodies of water, and I wanted her to always be with me when I went to the ocean.

To this day, every time I am in the ocean, wherever I am in the world, I feel Juliana's presence so deeply within me.

Chapter 3

In the months following Juliana's death, I experienced more heartache than I ever could have fathomed. After being strong for my daughter and family, I emotionally collapsed. I spent many days screaming into the pillow with anger, sadness, and helplessness. James had his own way of mourning: he completely shielded his aching heart from the world, including me. He made choices that were harsh toward me and almost destroyed me. He would get drunk and throw things around the house as he yelled at me, my brother, and my mom. He was so angry that he couldn't speak normally to me about anything pertaining to Juliana or money. He completely isolated me from his life, his feelings, and his thoughts. All I got were expressions of frustration, anger, and blame. There was no love left in his heart for anything or anyone and especially not for God. I was always walking on eggshells, fearing I'd say something or do something that would set him off. He was frustrated that we were back in my parents' house, back to being broke, and back to having nothing to smile about. He knew it wasn't my fault, and after major outbursts he would always say he was sorry. He was helpless, sad, and lost.

My parents were dealing with their own sorrow, and there was little energy left for me. My brother loved Juliana so much. He'd been her main babysitter. He couldn't even speak of what happened. Many of my friends couldn't bear to be around me because they felt guilty for being happy or celebrating. No one really understood how to act around me because I was, by nature, happy and upbeat. I didn't know how to be sad in public and show all my emotions. I felt very alone and isolated. With no job, I was home alone a lot and that needed to change.

I got a job at our local Macy's, just to get out of the house, but it ignited the feeling of loneliness even more. Every time I heard a crying or cooing baby or the sound of children laughing as they played hide-and-seek between the clothing racks, the excruciating pain in my stomach would debilitate me.

What has become of me? I wondered. *I have so many gifts and talents, but I am spending my days putting away clothing on racks. I have so much love and passion in me, but I am going to sleep next to a man who thinks I am feeling anything but that.*

James felt so much resentment toward me. He was drowning in feeling sorry for himself and had little energy to comfort me. No matter how hard I tried to be strong and optimistic, he only saw the worst in me. He no longer felt love for me or compassion. The tsunami of anger began to gain momentum, and what happened next put out the tiny flame within me that was gasping for oxygen, desperate to stay lit.

He told me he had an affair and gave zero excuses for it—no explanation, no reason. He said nothing. All I knew was that he'd had sex with another woman. To give it a "but" or a "because" would not make it any better or worse, so he didn't explain. I remember the day I found out. It was a windy day in November, three years almost to the day since we kissed for the first time. James got home from work and asked me to sit with him in the car; he had something to tell me. There was no preparation. It was blunt, sad, and—for the first time in months—heartfelt.

"I had sex with another woman."

I felt my whole world collapse around me, I felt dizzy, as if I was living yet another nightmare. I felt the life force within me leave my body, I felt dead.

I went to the store and bought five packs of cigarettes. I sat in my car for four hours, alone, staring at the speedometer, which showed zero—exactly what I had in my life. I thought about how it felt now that many of my nightmares and biggest fears had come true. I felt what it was like to hit rock bottom. How it couldn't get much worse than this. I had my hands on the steering wheel, ready to leave and drive to the end of the world. I watched the trees fighting the strong winds of fall. They lost their leaves, which swirled violently around me in little tornadoes. It was the first time in my life that I thought, *Lucky is the person who is dead.*

Then James got in the car on the passenger's side. I couldn't even look at him. All he said was, "I am sorry. I am so sorry."

Normally, a situation like this would have made me yell and scream. It would have brought out the devil in me, making me say things that were cruel in hope of killing him with my words. But this time, I didn't feel anything but numb. Ice began to cover my heart, crystallizing at enormous speeds, like a beautiful lake in a blisteringly cold winter.

All I could do was whisper, "Why? What is that you resent me for? What did I do to make you act in such a cruel way?"

He paused for a minute and said, "You left me alone with Juliana. I was there by myself, watching her die, because you couldn't bear to look at her heart stop. You left me when I needed you so badly to be with me, and you weren't. I can't forgive you for it, no matter how much I try to understand why you left me all alone with our dying daughter."

It wasn't reason enough to spit on our marital vows, but at least I finally understood why he resented me and hated me and why he looked at me as if I were dead to him. At this point in my life, I'd lost my daughter, one of the loves of my life, and now I was losing my other love, my husband. I could forgive my daughter for leaving; it was her fate, and I made peace with it. I wasn't angry with her because it wasn't her doing. But James, my rock, the last remainder of my little family—I couldn't bear it. The pain was his direct doing, and my naturally understanding nature was no longer able to cope.

We sat in silence, smoking one cigarette after another, speechless at what had become of us. What was I going to do? What were we going to do? What would become of our family? How would we rebuild our relationship? More important, could we rebuild it, and did we have the strength to rebuild it? All these questions danced in my head with the same force as the leaves dancing outside my windshield. Then, I asked James if he loved me and wanted to make it work. "Are you willing do everything to be with me?"

He promised to give me his all, to rebuild our relationship, and to give me plenty of reasons to stay. I was ready to divorce him, leave New Jersey, and find a new place to begin my new life. The thought of leaving everything behind actually excited me. I wanted to smell new air, see new things, and forget everything my life had been. I made no decisions that day. I was too tired, too sick, and too weak to think about what the next step would be.

The next few weeks were difficult. It was Christmas time, and watching the excited, smiling faces of children everywhere brought me a little bit of hope. I stood in line at J. C. Penney's, waiting to buy a beautiful candle, not for decoration but to light near the picture of my baby girl in remembrance. Not one person who commented on how beautiful the sparkling candle was had any idea what its purpose would be. The overwhelming tsunami of emotions now had enough velocity that the tidal wave could flood me, make me purge, and cleanse me and free me.

On Christmas Eve at my in-laws' house, the family rejoiced in my nephew's first Christmas, but I could no longer fake my smile. I asked James if we could leave early and go home. It made James really angry at me. He felt comforted by his family and the warmth of Christmas, but had I reached a breaking point and had little care for his desires. The pressure of my emotions and anger had finally reached a breaking point, and I needed to release all that was within me. On the way home, I said nothing. I was so overwhelmed with emotions that I had tried so hard to suppress. I had tried to put on a happy face and seem okay to everyone so that people wouldn't feel sorry for me or see me as weak. If I was weak or vulnerable, then I was not admirable.

These were the thoughts that caged me: the sadness of Christmas without our baby girl; the emptiness of life without Juliana's presence; the deep, dark, gaping hole in my heart from James's affair and betrayal; the sexual harassment I had to take at work in order to keep my job; the horrific financial anxiety my mother felt after losing her job, just days before Christmas; the loss of friends who didn't know how to behave around me; and the resentment I felt for James's sister, who had a child to hold when I didn't. All the emotions needed to be released.

We got home, and I lost all control. I wanted to hurt James so badly. I stood in my parents' living room and screamed at the top of my lungs, *"Why, why, why?"* I hit him with my fists as hard as I could—in his arm, his back, wherever I could. I felt so helpless. I couldn't take it anymore.

"Why did God take away my baby? Why did you fucking cheat on me? Why is this happening to me? Why are we living like fucking mice? Why does everything always fall apart? Why does God hate us so fucking much? Why can't we have a single fucking reason to smile about, just one good thing?" The sadness, anger, and feeling of being forsaken by God left me lying on the floor, crying, screaming, and barely breathing.

It was the first time since Juliana's diagnosis that I finally had a chance to break down and face the feelings I had tried so hard to suppress. It was the first time since that fateful day when I learned of James's affair that I had a chance to scream to the world, not just in my head. I finally understood the magnitude of what happened— Juliana, the affair, the degrading job I had. This was rock bottom, the lowest point of my life. It took a mere eight months of build up, and the release was only a few minutes long. I alternated crying on the floor with punching James in the arm, stomach, and anywhere I could. With each punch, I screamed, "Why, why, *why?*"

Then I'd had enough. I ran upstairs and packed James's stuff.

I was done. I was no longer going to allow people around me to destroy what little I had left within me. I was going to start fresh. I was going to begin a new life. And just like the story of Christmas, I experienced the birth of a new person within me. This new person was not going to take shit from anyone, including God himself! James was crying, begging me to let him stay, but I had no more feelings left—no anger, no sadness, and, more important, no love. I'd reached a threshold. I was dead but not yet buried.

He left, and I felt nothing. I shut off all emotions, and a part of me died. It hurt so bad, but I couldn't feel the pain. It felt so good to release, but I couldn't feel the relief. Feelings were my enemy, and they were no longer going to destroy me. I was tired of fighting the cards I was dealt, and I was tired of fighting to feel better. I was at peace. The house was quiet, lit by the lights flickering on the Christmas tree. Then, the doorbell rang. It was James, standing there in the freezing cold, his breath visible and covering his face. His eyes, the window to the soul, were broken. He'd come back, leaving behind his ego, his anger, his resentment, and all that made him evil. He came in, hugged me, and cried hysterically, soaking me in his tears. I felt nothing. Because of my lack of emotions, I didn't fight him on anything. He asked if we could talk, and I agreed, on the terms that we would allow each other to speak openly and honestly. I warned him that the conversation I was willing to have was not a sign that we were still together. He accepted my terms, and we walked to the garage, where we could smoke.

This was the night we got to know each other from the core and out, not out and to the core, as we did when we met. We sat in the garage for five hours, freezing and sweating, crying and laughing, all at the same time. I told him everything I'd wanted to tell him all these years. We told each other all the things that annoyed us about each other. I told him how much I wanted to experience in the world, how badly I wanted to travel, and how much I missed losing myself in tasting fine cuisine. When we met, I left a very luxurious lifestyle that I'd had with my previous boyfriend. James always looked down on people who were living fancy lifestyles, mainly because he never had a taste for that. I told him all my dreams. I was no longer embarrassed to say I wanted more out of life, I didn't fear that I would sound pretentious. James associated luxury with pretentious-bitch behavior. I told him I wanted a lavish lifestyle, including living in a gorgeous house and having as many kids as we wanted, not as many as we could afford, I wanted to live not paycheck to paycheck but with plenty of cash to live joy to joy. I told him how much I saw in him and his potential to be great and the disappointment I felt as I watched his self-esteem dwindle with one massive blow after another at work.

That night, he told me how much he really loved me. He told me what he really thought of me, not the reserved, cold behavior he had shown toward me. It was as if his pride had forbidden him to be kind and warm toward me. His security guards who stood in front of his ego, protecting him, left and allowed him to speak from the heart. He no longer desperately tried to protect his ego, image, and true being. I too asked my guards to leave, and I no longer filtered what my heart was trying to say to protect my own ego, which was controlled by my belief system of how I "should" be and not what I truly was.

We spoke our minds and were free to say what we honestly felt without seeming vulnerable or weak. We didn't argue; we spoke. We didn't belittle; we respected each other. We didn't resent one another; we loved, not as husband and wife but as human beings who shared a history. The road ahead was going to be long, but the cement truck was there to pour the foundation of our new home and our new relationship. The old house that was our relationship collapsed, as it had been built with a fast-paced passion instead of a deep understanding of love and of each other.

Now we were rebuilding, carefully laying brick after brick, one on top of the other with the intention of never being finished.

Chapter 4

New Year's Eve 2008

It was a week since our collapse, and we had spoken little. When we did, however, it was kind. My brother was offered a DJ gig at one of the most exclusive steakhouses in New York City. The admission price was four hundred dollars per person, an astronomical amount of money for us at the time. But as our angel Juliana would have it; the owner of the steakhouse, after hearing our story, offered to give us the best seat in the house for free.

On December 31, I often liked to take a long walk to reflect on the year and think of what I wanted to experience in the following twelve months. On my walk, I couldn't help but feel like I was connecting to a higher spirit. I truly and honestly felt like Juliana was, for the first time since her death, speaking to me through my soul. It was the single most important day of my life. I looked up at the sky and inhaled the crisp, cold air. While I was taking deep breaths, I suddenly had a thought: *How could the powers of the world unite to compel the cells that I am made of to merge and divide perfectly and to grow me so that I am a fully healthy, functioning human being, only to then forsake me, causing me to experience so much pain? No way, it can't be!*

I was brought into this world for a reason, and that reason can't solely be to suffer. I have been plagued with fearful thoughts and worry my entire life, and now that I had experienced most of my fears and survived them, I could get through anything! Those worries never prevented the horror that happened to me, no matter how many nights I stayed up worrying, especially about the well-being of my daughter. Those worrying, fearful thoughts might even have caused some of the events to happen. It was Juliana's fate to die, but not mine. I was meant to live. What would I do now with my newfound life? I had an amazing angel looking after me. I felt so safe and so empowered. I felt all the prayers of strength from all those who loved me permeate my body and soul. It was a new life and a new year, and I would begin the New Year with a clean slate.

I forgive James. I forgive God. I forgive everyone who has been unable to be there for me, I thought. *I forgive myself for wasting time and living in fear. I will no longer be a slave to my thoughts; I will be the owner of them. I can do anything. No amount of pain or failure can compare to what I have been through. I am bulletproof. I am strong. I deserve to live the life I've dreamed about. I am not alone. I will rebuild.*

A vision of a beautiful brick home came to me, and I opened the door, holding a baby in my arms as two little girls hugged my legs. It felt so real. I could smell the delicious air surrounding the house. I could see myself smiling, glowing, and happy. Golden rays of sunlight on a fall day blinded the image I had in my head. I felt the sky above me open and pour light into my soul. I felt one with God. I felt Juliana's love and felt so close to her. I felt her sweeping the pain away and flooding my body with enormous strength. When I thought of her, I no longer felt pain and tried to think about something else. I finally felt her as the light that she was—and is. I felt one with my vision and so empowered. I felt as if I had just come back from war and was being rewarded for my survival, bravery, and heroism. It was on this walk that the course of my life changed forever.

James and I drove to New York to celebrate the New Year, and as I looked out the window, I saw a new world. It was the same road I'd driven on when Juliana was being transferred to Hackensack

Medical, her last trip in a car, alive. Now, this was my first trip feeling truly alive, possibly for the first time in my life. The entire year had flashed before my eyes, and I was grateful for the lessons that, just a few hours before, had felt like punishments. The air smelled different, and my body felt different. My soul was at peace. At 11:59, I laid the year to rest, with pain yet relief that it was over. I swore to myself that I would not allow thoughts of pain, anger, and resentment to follow me into the new year or the rest of my life. At midnight, a light was born within me, and as I kissed James, that light began to grow.

***

The first week of 2009 felt fresh and exciting. James and I made love for the first time since he told me about his affair. It was an unusually magical night, one that brought much healing and renewed emotion. I couldn't stop thinking about why we were not getting pregnant; we'd been trying for almost a year at this point, and I made a doctor's appointment. During the visit early in February, the nurse asked me about my last period, and I couldn't remember the date. The doctor performed an ultrasound and confirmed that my uterine lining was very thick and needed to shed. He prescribed a pill that would help my uterus shed its lining, and thus, I would menstruate, helping my cycle to regulate. I held that prescription in my purse for days and then weeks, as if by some crazy force, I kept forgetting to fill it.

On February 17, 2009, I had a dream in which my beautiful Juliana came to visit me. She hadn't come to see me in months. The last time I dreamed about her she told me that the batteries in her breathing machine were dying, and she needed me to change them. I asked her to never visit me in the form of a nightmare again, and so she did as I asked. But on this particular night, she needed to give me a very important message. In the dream, we were in a beautiful park, and she was the same age that she would have been, had she lived—about eighteen months old. She had the most beautiful glowing face, rosy cheeks, and the brightest blue eyes. Her hair was long, and she was wearing a white dress. I hugged her and told her how much I missed her and how much I didn't want our time together to end. She never spoke to me; she only smiled. She hugged me and kissed my belly. At the moment she kissed my belly, I felt a strong heartbeat vibrate in my abdominal area. I woke up immediately and felt my heart pounding. Of course, I thought it was just my heartbeat that I'd felt in my dream.

I was new to this world of communicating with and merging with the other side. I was new to signs from my angel; I didn't quite believe in such signs or understand their meaning. Then, on March 1, I decided to go shopping for some larger clothing, as I had been feeling a little bloated. As I was driving, suddenly I felt someone tap me on the shoulder. I got so scared that I almost crashed the car. I felt like someone was in the car with me, and I kept looking at the backseat. It was a very scary experience, one that freaked me out so much I had to pull over. The only place to pull over was the parking lot of a CVS Pharmacy. After I stopped, I don't know what came over me, but I felt this push to go inside and buy a pregnancy test. I'd seen a new digital pregnancy test advertised on TV earlier that morning, the slogan of which was, "the most advanced piece of technology you will ever pee on." It stuck with me as I looked for a test in the store. I bought it and decided to go back home to see what this "advanced piece of technology" would detect.

After I took the test, it seemed to take forever to give me a reading. I had taken many tests in the last nine months, and they were all sadly negative. After every negative result, it would take me days to stop feeling sad and sometimes even broken. Then, as I was washing my hands, I looked down and saw the read-out: *pregnant*.

Oh my goodness, I thought. *I can't believe this. I am pregnant. I will be a mother again! I am not broken. I am worthy. I am going to finally hold a baby. We will be a family again.* Suddenly, I felt the clouds above my head disperse just enough to let me feel the warmth of a tiny ray of sunlight. I grabbed the test and ran over to my dad.

"Papa, I'm pregnant! I am *pregnant*! Oh, my God!" We hugged and jumped up and down, overwhelmed with excitement.

I called James to tell him the wonderful news. We had tried for more than a year to get pregnant, so to finally say the words "I am pregnant" to James was an amazing reason to rejoice. I prayed that I would be with child when we visited the beautiful place where we sprinkled Juliana's ashes on the one-year anniversary of her passing, which was only seventeen days away. James was tearfully overjoyed, and he came home with the biggest, most beautiful bouquet of tulips; they filled three large vases. Life was starting to look up for us. Within the first eight weeks of the year, we were able to find better, higher-paying jobs closer to home and also to conceive a beautiful child.

The shift that happened within me on New Year's Eve also was shifting the world around me showing me an entirely new universe, one that loved and served me, instead of punishing and forsaking me. It was then that I fully began to understand the power of my thoughts and emotions. When I stopped feeling sorry for myself, the universe stopped giving me circumstances that would give me reasons to self-loathe.

An amazing moment was when I went to the doctor, and he confirmed that I was almost nine weeks pregnant. More important to me, I was about five weeks pregnant when Juliana came to kiss my belly. It's at that time that the heart begins to beat in the womb. To receive a gift directly from her left me feeling so loved. The next few months were filled with daily reasons to smile and celebrate. We had little money and little to eat—the 2009 financial crisis left my mom without a job and my dad struggling with his own business—but the vision of our future felt so real that it created the same excitement within us as if the future was already happening. James was working seven days a week, trying to learn about his new business venture, which was privatizing a state-mandated insurance called temporary disability benefits (TDB) by moving clients from the state to a private insurance carrier. It was a lot of work, and he was starting from scratch. He had the "nothing to lose" mentality because we couldn't have gotten any worse than we were. All we talked about was our future—our dream life. We would spend our weekends driving through gorgeous neighborhoods, envisioning ourselves living in the stunning homes and enjoying abundance in all aspects of life. As we drove around, we would hold hands and squeeze really tight when we saw the house of our dreams. We attempted to contain our excitement, as if we were moving in tomorrow. As funny as it seems now, it was the only way we could have gone through the difficult growing pains of business and family. When you live in your dreams, you begin to enjoy the perks of already being there long before reality catches up.

My pregnancy progressed beautifully, and I felt amazing. On our way to find out the sex of the baby and if it was developing properly, James turned to me and said, "What if we don't find out the sex? Let's keep it a surprise. Who cares, anyway, as longs as the baby is healthy?"

At first, I felt I needed to know, but then I realized he was right. It made no difference at all. Nothing would change if we found out now, and it wasn't as if we could afford to start buying baby stuff. We had just enough to buy food and help my parents pay the mortgage. We spent the remainder of the pregnancy in excitement, wondering every day who we might have. It was at that time when I began to fully trust and test Juliana. I asked her for a girl and then thought, *Let's see if she heard me or if she has any power.* James was certain it was a boy, and we were going to call him Benjamin (like the name of the steakhouse on New Year's Eve where we had our "rebirth").

On October 7, three days before my due date, I felt contractions all night. They weren't painful, just annoying. At five o'clock that morning, I told James we needed to go to the hospital, as I felt very steady contractions. We arrived at the hospital, which was in Princeton, New Jersey. We'd spent every Sunday in Princeton with Juliana, enjoying walks and ice cream. We had not been back since the last time we were there with her, a few weeks before her diagnosis. It felt amazing to be back in Princeton. I was hours away from being a mother again.

We checked into the hospital, but unfortunately, I had not progressed as far as I had hoped. I so badly wanted to have a vaginal delivery, after the C-section I had with Juliana. I tried to be strong and wait for progress, but then the doctor came in. He was not very supportive of my VBAC (vaginal birth after cesarean), or rather, it was a Thursday, and he had a bar mitzvah to go to later that day. As James and I squealed with excitement about being parents again, the doctor told James, "She should just have the C-section. You can hold your baby in about two hours. Why go through labor and risk not even successfully VBAC-ing?"

Of course, when you tell a man who has longed to be a father that he can hold his baby within hours, his patience with my long labor ran short. To be honest, so had mine. This decision, however, would have a huge impact on my life for the next three years.

I was prepped for the surgery, and as I lay on the table, I closed my eyes and prayed. As my baby transitioned from heaven to life, I made sure my energy was flooded with love, joy, and gratitude. My mind was clear, and I was calm as I waited to hear the first cry. Then I felt a little pressure, and the doctor announced, "It's a beautiful baby ... girl!"

I can still hear his voice in my head when I think back to that moment. *Thank you, thank you, thank you*, I thought. I was the mother of a baby girl again, just what I secretly wanted. The nurses wrapped her and gave me a few seconds to nuzzle her. Her face was so warm and soft. I felt my heart flood with bliss. My dream, my vision, had finally come true.

I love naming babies by honoring those I love so dearly. My mother's name is Ludmila, and I had to honor Juliana, so we took the last four letters of my mother's name and last two letters of Juliana's to come up with Milana. I love her name, and it gave me great joy to honor my mother and Juliana, my greatest sources of love.

When I finally arrived in my room, the nurses brought her to me. James and I couldn't stop smiling. We were parents again to a beautiful baby girl! I looked at her almost in disbelief; she was finally here. All I wanted to do was kiss her and hold her close, inhale her, and comfort her. Our parents came to visit us, and I could feel the dark cloud that had plagued our family spread apart, and the warm rays of sunlight embraced us, healing us and strengthening our souls.

Milana and I were inseparable. I spent a lot time reading Dr. Sears's books on attachment parenting. He wrote a lot about giving your all to your baby, and his ideas resonated with me. Holding my baby as often as possible, building a strong bond, and being "one" with my child were all ideas I felt strongly about. His books helped me, but sometimes I felt obsessed with making her happy, no matter the toll it took on me. While James was out building his insurance agency, Milana and I were home. I felt so lucky to be in my old bedroom because I didn't have to be apart from her. There was only one place to sleep, and that was next to me. I didn't have to explain to James why the baby was in our bed; it was obvious, and he couldn't really protest. I loved sleeping with her, and being in one room made it really easy to do that. We would spend our days going on walks, snuggling, nursing, and sleeping. It was an amazing time in my life ... for the first few weeks.

Then, as I began to take out Juliana's clothing for the new baby, feelings of anxiety started to surface. I was confused—was this Juliana again? Did I really live through losing her? Why didn't she feel the same way? Why couldn't I feel anything? Where did my emotions go? I watched James snuggle her, and I blurted out, "You love her? Like, you feel love for her?"

He looked at me like I was crazy. "Of course," he said as he proceeded to kiss her all over.

Oh, my goodness! I can't feel anything, I thought. Adding to my anxiety was that Milana refused a bottle or pacifier. She also had acid reflux and needed to be held upright in a body wrap for most of the day. I began to feel like I was suffocating, I couldn't step out of the house alone, and the feeling of shackles holding me down was incredibly difficult for me to deal with. The guilt overwhelmed me; not only did I have a "difficult" baby, but I also was unable to feel, not even instinctively. At first, I thought I was experiencing baby blues, but the more research I did, the more I realized there was a lot more going on inside me.

When I attempted to suppress pain, with that I also suppressed joy. At the time, I didn't know that I couldn't prevent myself from feeling pain and only allow feelings of joy to come in. Feelings, good or bad, come from the same place, and there needs to be an opportunity to express both. My way of coping with the pain of losing a baby and my husband's betraying my trust was to not deal with feeling. I just diverted my attention to something else. I tried to be positive and find distractions or reasons to not feel what I was feeling. That trick eased the pain for the moment and thus suppressed my ability to feel anything at all. I figured if I didn't feel pain, that was a great way to be. I didn't realize that over time, I would lose the ability to feel altogether. I was still able to feel happy, and I genuinely smiled during joyful moments, but to truly feel happiness was another emotion.

I now know that problems and emotions are meant to teach us something by bringing up something that needs to be addressed. I didn't understand this back then, so I did what I was good at: I put negative emotions into the recycling bin in my subconscious. Recycled items do not disintegrate. They are packed down and made into objects that often have no resemblance to their original form. Such is the nature of problems. When they resurface, they often morph into completely different issues, creating anxiety that seems to stem from a bottomless hole. (I will get back to this later in the story when things got really ugly.)

On top of everything, Milana was different from the happy-with-everything baby that Juliana was ... and I began to miss her dearly. I felt depressed about not having a natural birth and failing to stick with my desire to feel a baby come through me, something I felt such a deep desire to experience. I felt like my body was broken. Why couldn't my body just "work"? I was beginning to crash, mentally and physically, from being frustrated with guilt over my lack of feelings, as well as the amount of care Milana required of me.

As my negative emotions toward my body began to snowball, my milk supply began to dwindle. Thank God I was unable to afford formula and thus was forced to do a lot of research on how to bring up my supply. I found that negative feelings toward one's body can often affect the milk supply. The more I worried about how much milk I was *not* making, the less milk I made.

I began to change my thinking of having a broken body that couldn't successfully labor and birth a baby to positive thoughts, such as, *My body is perfect for growing a life inside me. That is all I could ever ask for.* As I nursed as often as every hour, I would close my eyes and envision my breasts as rivers overflowing with milk. The more grateful I felt for my body, the more milk I began to produce. But even though I dealt with the issue of feeding my daughter, other things caused anxiety within me.

I wanted a home I could call my own. It wasn't easy living under the same roof with my entire family. Though I love them to pieces, I wanted to live on my own terms with my little family. At Christmastime, when Milana was about three months old, it was a time of healing, and my thoughts began to change. Just a year prior, I was devastated by not having a baby and by thoughts of divorce. That contrast reminded me of how many of my dreams did come true. I truly was lucky to hold a baby once more.

One evening, while everyone was gone, Milana and I sat by the Christmas tree, enjoying the lights illuminating the room. The fire was going, and the warmth of the burning wood made me feel as if my angel had come to see me again. I was nursing Milana, and as she looked up at me, staring deep in to my eyes, I felt her eyes pierce my soul. I could feel that she had so much love and gratitude toward me. I had tried so hard to give her the happiest life. I tried so hard to nurse her as often as she asked, and I held her for hours … and she was grateful to me for trying. That moment ignited feelings again, and tears poured from my eyes. My tears dropped on Milana's face, and the tickling sensation made her smile. After the tears of pain, I began to shed tears of joy. I felt again all the emotions that I'd suppressed. I purged. I felt guilty for wanting Juliana back. I felt guilty for not fully accepting Milana. I felt guilty for not feeling happy because I had another baby. I felt guilty for feeling guilty. But now that I purged my emotions, I had space for love and joy. Though the ice that surrounded my emotions melted just a bit, at least I didn't feel *nothing*.

My dearest baby girl's smiling, grateful eyes that twinkled by the fire healed me in ways I still feel today. I held her in my arms long after she fell asleep, as I thought about the last few years. I finally realized that I had become a mother again. I was privileged to have a second chance, and this time my baby was healthy. She was breathing on her own, and she was not tied down to machines. She was free to be held and fed and to experience the wonder of babyhood. While Juliana was sick, I longed to hold her. Now, Milana wanted nothing else but to be in my arms—to snuggle, to sleep, to live.

I realized that I got exactly what I'd wanted; I got a baby who wanted only to be in my arms. I was beginning to break through again, but it would take another year for me to finally break free of my mommy guilt.

Chapter 5

New Year's Eve 2009 was exactly one year to the day since my last epiphany. I thought about everything the year had brought me. I was so grateful for becoming a mother again, for James and his keeping his promise to give us a better life, and for Juliana's daily miracles. Not a day went by without something beautiful happening unexpectedly, just to bring a smile to my heart. I felt that random acts of kindness from strangers or friends were messages of love from Juliana. I thought about how far I'd come in just twelve months, and I felt empowered to plan the next twelve months. I had a vision of us moving into a home we could call our own. I saw us living without much worry about money. I felt the freedom to make choices that only financial abundance can give. I began to truly believe in dreaming and in the power of visualizing what I wanted. I felt like I was finally able to grasp how the course of my life would run. Every day I would take Milana in the stroller and walk for two or sometimes three hours. On those walks, I mentally created the life I wanted to live. After months of visualizing, I felt all the feelings of already living the dream. I just had to make it a reality.

On our first New Year's Eve as a family again, we spent the evening with our nearest dearest friends and family. As the clock stuck twelve, I felt a renewed energy within me, and I looked at the world around me with new eyes. Milana and I had grown closer and closer; my love for her deepened every day. I learned to deal with my emotions as I felt them so that they would not again subside into my emotional "recycling bin," only to surface again at another time.

It was a freezing cold January day, and the snow was coming down hard. Milana and I just lay in bed, watching the snow dance outside the window. I felt so close to her. She wrapped her arm around my neck, holding me close. It was in that moment that I realized how much love she felt for me and how happy she was just being near me. I believe God gives us children to awaken every blissful feeling within us. We belong in a blissful state; it is our birthright, and children make it easy to feel this euphoric sensation.

As I looked at Milana's deep blue eyes, I could see God. All that was good in the world was in her eyes, I felt so blessed that I was chosen as the person to bring this beautiful soul into the world. I realized that all her unusual attachments were not coming from a place of control or manipulation. They were coming from an innate desire to almost force me to build a bond with her and to not be afraid of getting attached. She felt me so deeply and gave me exactly what I needed—time to snuggle, to hold her, to feel her aura and energy heal me, and to strengthen my belief in the miracle that is her existence. I stopped trying to teach her independence; she could depend on my being there whenever she needed me. She initiated our closeness and built our relationship. In retrospect, it was her need to be held and nursed every two hours that brought us closer. I often wonder how different our relationship would be today, had I made the choice to go back to working full time. Her healing energy reignited so much love and joy within me. She needed me to be near her at all times so that she could work her magic. I am eternally grateful to her for all she has given me.

On May 4, 2010, James came home around ten o'clock in the evening. Smiling and excited, he handed me a card he'd made out of printing paper that read,

"To you. From me."

"We have something special to celebrate! Happy anniversary, babe. I love you."

I felt like a giddy little girl, as if I'd just received a note from a boy in class. As we stood in the kitchen, hugging and kissing on our third wedding anniversary, James whispered in my ear. "Babe, I have a special surprise for you. Tell your mom to watch Milana. I want to take you somewhere to celebrate." I couldn't stop smiling with excitement. Where could he possibly want to take me so late in the evening? As we left the house, my parents stood in the doorway. waving good–bye.

"Hve fun, guys, and happy anniversary!" my mom yelled out. As we began to drive, James reached for my hand and gave it a squeeze. The drive was about forty minutes, and I don't think we said one word to each other. We just enjoyed holding hands and listening to music. I didn't even ask where we were going. I didn't care; I was so happy to just be alone with him, thinking about the last three years of our marriage. Then we arrived at a little beach town called Sea Bright, the town where James had his office. I loved this heavenly little town. I spent the majority of my last trimester pregnant with Milana, cooling off on the beautiful beaches there. But I was confused as to why we were there.

"Babe, what are we doing here? Everything is closed," I said.

"Don't worry," James said, smiling.

We pulled into the driveway of a beautiful townhome—a mansion for me at the time—and I yelled at him that we would get in trouble for trespassing. He laughed as he got out of the car, walked up to the security key pad, and opened the garage door. My mouth dropped to my lap; my heart was pounding from excitement. He opened my door, extended his hand to help me out, and said, "Welcome home, babe. Happy anniversary." I jumped up and down, hugging him, almost knocking him over.

We walked upstairs and before our eyes was the most beautiful kitchen I had ever seen—cabinets the color of golden honey, gorgeous granite countertops and backsplash, stunning hardwood floors, and top-of-the-line stainless-steel appliances. The ceilings were ten feet high with decorative moldings. I couldn't believe what I was seeing, and then we went upstairs. The master bedroom had a massive ceiling. The windows on the left offered a view of the ocean; the windows on the right gave a glimpse of the Shrewsbury River. The sun would rise and set from the windows in that room—my dream bedroom!

Everything was magnificent, but I'd known every single inch of this house before I was in it. Months prior, I found this townhome online, and I fell in love with it. It was way too expensive for us at the time, but I used to look at the pictures and envision myself there. I would stare at those pictures to escape my living situation. I would fall asleep, thinking of how I would decorate the townhouse—the type of curtains those beautiful windows needed and the way I would set up the furniture. I had every detail planned out in my head. At the time, it was just a way to escape my sometimes-anxious thoughts. Now, I would move into the house I loved and that I'd made a home of in my imagination—that exact house!

How that happened is an incredible series of events. The housing market crashed, and the builder of the home wanted to wait out the epic drop in home prices and rent it out. He didn't have much of a mortgage on it, so any amount of money would do. A few weeks prior to moving in, we were invited to a birthday party for James's business partner, and, as fate would have it, we sat next to the guy who owned that house. Unbeknownst to me, James told him about our living situation, and he found it in his heart to rent us the house for a mere $1,300 a month, with no down payment. The deal was that as we made more money, we would pay more each month, but for now, we had a place to call home.

The address was 17 New Street. The number seventeen was the worst number for me since it was the day Juliana passed away. I know this house was all her doing since she knew I would relate seventeen to her, and the street was named New. I took it as a sign that it was a new beginning for us and a new interpretation of the number seventeen.

One of the greatest gifts that home gave us was the view of

the ocean, a place where our beautiful Juliana rests. What a lovely reminder that she is with us all the time. Every morning, the first thing I saw was Milana's sleeping face and then a glimpse of the ocean, where my other baby was. I felt like I had them both together, near me, loving me, and me loving them.

The course of our lives changed on that very day, and we never looked back. James's quest for an opportunity to build a profitable business had finally come to fruition. Though the initial payoff was small, after working seven days a week from morning to night, the business began to grow, and so did the money in our bank account.

We moved into the townhouse just as the sweetness of spring filled the air. Living a block away from the beach was amazing; we spent every evening spread out on a blanket, enjoying the sunsets, eating dinner, and rejoicing in this new life God had bestowed upon us. I spent many hours walking the beach with Milana in my carrier; she was seven months at the time of our move. The salt air would put her to sleep for hours, and I loved holding her, smelling her, and dreaming of the future with the utmost optimism. Every day began with a long walk in the neighboring town, a heavenly place called Rumson. Picturesque gigantic trees lined the streets, and all the properties overflowed with flowers and stunning landscaping. A major shift in energy within me put me in a never-ending feeling of bliss, gratitude, and joy. It was easy to feel amazing when I was so close to the ocean. Knowing that Milana would grow up in this delicious fresh air made me feel like I was doing something so wonderful for her. She blossomed every day. The sun kissed her beautiful face, and her eyes twinkled with excitement every time I looked at her.

Every day, I felt Juliana's love all around me, especially when I got a glimpse of the ocean. My belief in her as our guarding angel deepened with each passing day. I began to see little miracles all around me, and I thanked her many times throughout the day. Things always worked out in the best way for us. The more I reached out to her from a place of love, the more she responded with reasons to deepen my love for the life around me. I had crazy thoughts—like, she chose me to be her mother to establish a deep bond, and then she left me because she could do so much for me from the "other side" than in the earth plane. Sometimes I would feel guilty for thinking such thoughts, but the more I did, the happier I felt, and feelings of being forsaken ultimately subsided completely. I felt as if a higher power was always looking after me, giving me the feeling of being protected and looked after.

One warm September day in 2010, shortly before Milana's first birthday, James texted me: "We have to talk when I get home." A few hours later I heard footsteps on the stairs and a friendly "Hi, babe."

"Hey, love, how was your day?" I asked. "So what is that we have to talk about?"

"Babe, you know that I studied criminal justice in college and always wanted to be a cop. Well, the Sea Bright Police Department is going to sponsor my attending the police academy for the entire nine months!" He spoke with more excitement than I had ever heard.

"Oh, what about the business? You're not going to get rid of it, are you?"

"No, I'm going to work all day and do the academy training at night.",

"So you're going to be a cop? I thought you were over that dream."

"Well, yeah, I was but I'm thinking of doing it on the side. Cops work four days on and four days off. Babe, this is just for benefits and to have a backup plan, in case the insurance thing doesn't work out."

"Okay, as a backup plan. I didn't sign up to marry a cop. The anxiety of your possibly getting killed in the line of duty would put me on medication!" I burst out laughing, trying to make light of the situation, though deep down inside I was kind of pissed at him for taking on so much.

"Don't worry; I won't die." He laughed.

Truth is, I was proud of him for pursing his dream of being a cop, though deep down I knew he wasn't cop material; this was just something he wanted to experience.

Over the next nine months, James basically relinquished his title of father, husband, son, and friend so that he could pursue his dream. He left for work at 8:00 a.m., came home at 4:30, had a quick dinner, and left at 5:15 for the academy, returning home at 11:30 p.m. The days were long for him, and it certainly took a toll on his mental and physical well-being. What he thought was a dream became a nightmare. He was consumed with work and school, with no time for himself and especially not for us. On weekends he would often express his frustration by arguing with me over little things, sometimes even yelling and screaming like an angry child. It would end with him breaking down in tears, helpless and confused about his emotions. He was the architect of the life he was living. He'd chosen to start a business and do the work to move up in life. He chose to attend the police academy, so why were his choices the source of so much resentment?

I was raising our daughter almost entirely by myself, giving him this opportunity to do what he wanted. I supported him in every way and took care of everything that I could to take additional responsibilities off his plate, but it did nothing to alleviate his stress and frustration. As he spent the majority of his time away from me, the loneliness caused me to descend into the dark place within me that I used to called home.

By late October, the once sunny, sweet-smelling beach town turned into a deserted, cold, windy ghost town—not a soul on the streets, not a glimpse of blue in the sky, and constant bitterly cold winds that could knock you off your feet—and it began to take a toll on me. I was alone with a toddler all day with no car and no human beings to interact with. Weeks would go by, and my only interaction with adults consisted of brutal, angry outbursts during arguments with James, every single weekend. Every Friday, I couldn't wait to spend time with James, to get out of the house and see the world outside of the townhouse, but every Sunday, I couldn't wait for

Monday to come so that I could be left alone with Milana and our own peaceful routine. I was losing my joy. I felt like I was caged within my own life, and I had no choice but to weather the storm.

On weekends, there was little interaction between James and Milana. He would try to play with her but didn't know how—there was a special approach to her that only I knew. She needed time to get used to him after five days of not seeing him. Her detachment from James angered him even more. He didn't have the time or energy to cultivate a relationship with her, and so it was a never-ending battle. He would get angry that when he asked her to play with him, she would run to me, not wanting any part of him. I know that hurt him. He was working his ass off to give her an amazing life, but all she did was run away.

My daily joy was Milana. She kept me busy with games and daily dance parties. We had an amazing bond; we shared a similar sense of humor and found joy in watching the same movies. We were attached in every sense of the word. We did everything together—sleeping, eating, bathing. Her soul was so deep and so wise that she could feel me and read me so clearly—the perfect companion during a somewhat lonely time for me.

I dedicated myself completely to Milana. She was what the books referred to as a "high-needs child." She needed to nurse every two hours until she was about eighteen months old, though thinking back, nursing was the easy thing to do during times when I needed rest. She never accepted any food unless it came from the warmth of my breast—she never, ever took a bottle. She needed to play with me, not by herself. She needed all of my attention and demanded that I hold her almost all of the time. But amid this high need, I realized she was also unusually sensitive to my emotions, as I was to hers. She had an amazing gift of feeling what I was feeling and had the urge to hug me, kiss me, and shower me with her love. It seemed like the more I gave her what she wanted, the more she reciprocated. She was my mirror. When I was smiling, she was smiling; when I was laughing, she was laughing; and when I was feeling down, she would frown. She would never go to sleep without me, even during the day. I used to get so frustrated with her because I needed to get things done around the house, and I had little opportunity to do anything when she was awake. But then one day, after an hour and half of trying to help her sleep on her own, I looked at her adorable face and laughed.

I laughed because I understood that I was battling a child who knew damn well what she wanted and had no plans to budge. I was trying to put my foot down and be the parent who said "No, you will sleep by yourself." I quickly understood that my saying "You will sleep alone because I have to clean" did not make me a parent in control. It actually was my losing control over myself and reacting with frustration. She was a little more than a year old, but she was so sure of how she wanted to spend her naps and nights—on her mama with a breast in her mouth. Instead of fighting her, I began to embrace her desire to never be apart from me. No one ever wanted to be with me so badly, and it was actually a very nice feeling to be her everything, especially when James was not ever around. So what if the dishes didn't get washed, and my socks would stick to the grime on the floors? Was it really more important than giving my sweet little baby the snuggles she loved so much?

Even though I was in awe of the privilege of watching my daughter grow up before my eyes, my heart ached for more. There was more to me than just cleaning, cooking, doing laundry, and being the primary friend, food, and comforter of a toddler. Surely there was a way to balance my roles. After all, besides being a mother, a woman, a friend, a wife, a daughter, and a sister, I was also a human being who desired to share my ideas with the world. But my intense desire to give my daughter my all and to give her the happiest life possible overruled my desire to get out and be with the world. She was my happy place when reality sometimes was gloomy.

I never gave her to my parents for the night. I was worried that she would feel like I'd abandoned her, and I was obsessed with her happiness. It was that obsession that made me forget who I was—my desires and dreams and especially my relationship with James. Living solely for Milana, I drifted farther from my own needs, even when they ached to be heard. I suppressed thoughts of going on dates with James to talk about us, about him, and about me. I suppressed the desire to go out with my girlfriends to have a drink or enjoy an adult conversation. I couldn't fathom leaving Milana with anyone!

The more my obsession with Milana's happiness deepened, the farther away I got from myself. It was easier for me to make her happy than to make myself happy. Every time the anxiety would surface and crave my attention, I would shut it up for a few moments. The voice would quiet down, but it never stopped nagging. What my gut was trying to tell me was that I was born for something big. I was born to do something on a global scale, but I had no idea what that would be. I was torn between wanting to be an amazing mother and wife and wanting to pursue my own personal dreams. This battle of desires would continue to cause much of the anxiety and confusion I felt about the course of my life. I would sometimes lie awake in the middle of the night, wondering what I would be when I was no longer engulfed in responsibilities for a small child.

December was a beautiful time in our home. It was hard to argue when the home was lit up with the beauty of Christmas tree lights. We watched every Christmas cartoon and movie ever released. Milana and I danced to Christmas music, which was on replay in our house all day long. It was too cold and windy to go outside, and I'd given my parents my car. James and I didn't communicate much, but we did force ourselves to quiet our resentment toward each other, at least for a little while.

On New Year's Eve 2010, I spent the day thinking about how many of my dreams did come true, even though I still was waiting for many to come to fruition. I sat on the floor in our living room, watching Milana dance around with a huge smile on her face as she really got into *Frosty the Snowman.*

An amazing feeling came over me as I thought about how far we'd come. Just a few years earlier, I was living in a ten-foot-by-ten-foot hospital room, watching my daughter die a little bit every day. I would have given everything to be where I was right then—on the floor, laughing with my beautiful, healthy daughter. In many ways, I was basking in the light that once seemed to be at the end of a very long tunnel. I prayed in gratitude for the wonderful home we had to call our own. Though it housed many of our worst arguments, it also was the place of many awe-inspiring moments. Milana had taken her first steps on the floors of that house and had danced her first dances. The year 2010 had begun in survival mode and ended in an enormous desire to truly live and find myself and especially to feel the freedom to voice my deepest feelings. Something was brewing within me. I didn't know it at the time, but the seed for finding my purpose, aside from mothering, had been planted.

I thought about what I wanted out of 2011. I had visions of a closer relationship with James, in which I was living from my heart rather than constantly being controlled by my ego. I wanted so badly to let go of the anxiety of letting Milana spend more time with my parents so that I could have more fun outside of the home. I yearned to find a way to tend to my roles other than mother, which had been on the back burner for too long. I realized that my giving myself fully to Milana, while ignoring the much-needed alone time with James, ultimately would lead to divorce. Divorced parents who did little to work on their relationship would not contribute to Milana's happiness. But my biggest goal was to finally listen to my gut that had been screaming to be heard, and its voice was getting louder and louder. I would spend the entire year deciphering the messages that I received from my soul … and that's when things got very interesting.

I didn't know how to tend to myself—I hadn't done it in so long—but by January 2011, I knew that step one was to sign up for a gym membership. I needed to work out. I needed to release pent-up frustration on a treadmill. My thoughts always flowed easily out of my heart when I was running. I found a gym that had a daycare and even made a friend on my block, with whom I would catch a ride every morning. Funny how things work out when you just send the signal of desire to the universe; funny how quickly it responds and offers solutions.

By February, my friend was no longer sticking the her New Year's resolution to work out, which meant I didn't have a ride. I woke up on the morning of my birthday and enjoyed an amazing breakfast with my brother, James, and Milana. James went to work, and my brother and I spent the day enjoying each other's company. At around five o'clock, a loud knock on the door startled us. We quickly ran downstairs, but no one was there … but there was a key on the stoop and a brand-new Toyota Highlander was in the driveway. *Oh my goodness*, I thought. *I just got a car for my birthday!* Amazing how a simple commodity like a car can give such an enormous amount of freedom. *Thank you, universe, and thank you, James, for being so good to me.* Such a thoughtful gift reignited my love for James, though money was still a bit tight. It made me see how deep his heart really was, even though on the outside he appeared harsh and abrasive.

In March, I spent my days in going to the park and the mall and seeing the world around me. I was beginning to realize that I need to get away for some "me" time. From the day Milana was born, I hadn't had any time with my friends. I hadn't been out dancing or enjoying the freedom to travel alone. Milana was now eighteen months and still nursing, but I wasn't anxious about leaving her without milk. I finally mustered up the strength to tell James.

"I am going to Miami for the weekend to visit Natasha."

And just like with everything else in life that we overthink and feel we are not worthy of, James smiled and said, "Awesome. Go have fun. Milana and I will have a blast together."

Wait … what? James was going to stay with our child—whose only alone time with her had been while I took a shower—for a whole weekend, *and* he was excited about it? Had I thought myself in to a hole of loneliness, helplessness, and hopelessness? Did I do that to myself? All this time I thought I was a heroic mother who would never leave her child's side to tend to her selfish needs. In reality, I was doing destroying myself all on my own. No one appreciated it;

no one would think more of me or less of me if I spoke up about my needs and desires. I sat on the couch, thinking about how much I barricaded my world with thoughts that I'd created myself. I didn't need to be so obsessed with Milana's happiness to impress anyone, including Milana.

The guilt I felt over not feeling anything for her when she was born is what fueled my obsession with making her happy— I'd do anything so she wouldn't find out how I truly felt when she born. So I overcompensated for those feelings of guilt with insane determination that I would make her happy, loved, and content. But more so, I wanted so badly to show my parents what an extraordinary mother I was, never needing help or a night out. Someone mentioned in passing, "A mother is not a horse; a horse gets tired." That phrase was me exactly. I needed to show James that while he was out, productively building his company, I was home, productively building the perfect child, even if it was at the sacrifice of myself. It was then that I began to understand that my happiness is an inside job for which I am fully responsible. Once I found it, nourished it, and lived it, my daughter, husband, and parents would directly benefit from it.

Children don't ever tell their mothers, "Thank you for sacrificing your happiness and your needs so that you could perfectly tend to me." It was then that I realized how much Milana loved me, and for her to see me depressed because I was lacking a social life was not a joy to her. All she ever wanted was for me to be happy, just as I did for her. This realization was what my gut had been trying to convey to me all these months.

On the plane to Miami, my anxiety suddenly went away. Three days of fun, dancing, having cocktails by the pool, and enjoying my friends' company was so empowering. It was the birth of a new me—the "me" I had forgotten and had shushed all these years. No one offered help, simply because they didn't want to upset me by making me think I couldn't do this on my own. It wasn't that they didn't want to. My mother had told me she would love to take

Milana for the weekend while James and I enjoyed ourselves. James would offer help, but I was too obsessed with impressing him with my heroic ability to do it all. So everyone left me alone so that I could remain a "hero."

On the way home, I thought about what I really wanted to do, and I mentally designed how I wanted my days to go. I wanted to get out of the house. I wanted to travel. I wanted to enjoy my life with balance. I wanted to enjoy our new money by eating fine food, going on amazing vacations, and wearing clothing that made me feel like a million bucks. I now felt I was worthy of it all.

Chapter 6

In April, my newfound self came with a lot of blowouts with James. I was sick of smiling through the weekly mood swings, stiff face, and cold-as-hell energy that permeated his being. The picture of our living in a nice home, looking beautiful, with a gorgeous, perfect little girl was in a pretty frame. I held on to that picture in my head, hoping it was real and true, but no matter how hard I tried, it wasn't. Things only began to take a turn when I took that beautifully framed picture and smashed it to pieces. I no longer would strive to be the perfection I saw in that family picture so vividly in my head. I was going to strive to be real and be what we were. I was going to begin living from a place of reality, not a place of perfection that I'd mainly created as an escape. *I wasn't perfect when I lost my child,* I thought, *but now look at me!* Only then was I able to finally speak the thoughts I was holding inside. My desire to appear strong in James's eyes was my biggest obstacle.

On a windy Sunday morning during breakfast, James just got up and left. I don't know what triggered it; I don't know what was said, and later, when I asked him, he didn't know himself. I calmly smiled at Milana as tears drenched my face. What the fuck was happening? It was time to address our problems; it was time to have the talk and decide if we would stay together or part ways. I couldn't live like this anymore and continue to put sparkles on everything, solely to survive in peace. I didn't want peace anymore; it was temporary. I wanted a breakthrough, a decision, an answer, an outcome. I wanted to end the horrific atmosphere in the house whenever James was home. *I didn't sign up for this*, I thought. *I deserve so much more.*

I took Milana to the park to get some air so I could think about what I would say and do if we couldn't resolve this. Moving back with my parents seemed like the best and safest option. To leave was the easiest option. I hated confrontation. I hated talking about what I was thinking about. I liked to sweep things under the rug. I just wanted peace … but at what price? It took all the strength I had to finally face my reality, face the facts, and do something about our constant head-to-head wars. At this point, inaction was a lot more painful than the action itself—the action of taking off my "happy with everything" mask and telling the truth about how miserable I was.

James texted me to come home. I took a deep breath and felt my heart beating so hard that I felt nauseated. I put Milana down for a nap when we got home, and then I went out on the balcony, where James was waiting. I looked at his face; he looked so tired and as if he'd been crying. I let my guard down and felt compelled to let him speak until there was nothing left to say.

He told me that the police academy was once his biggest dream, but just days into his training, he realized it was one of his biggest mistakes. He hated being degraded every day—he was treated like a piece of shit, and the constant yelling in his face from the drill sergeant made his blood boil. He wore a suit to work every day and had a big, beautiful office with employees. He was doing deals with top politicians by day and getting belittled by night. He felt guilty for leaving us and for missing out on his daughter's milestones and the chance to build a relationship with her because of the choices he made. Yet every day he was away from us, he was investing his time, and he felt he couldn't leave. If he left, after all the time he'd put in, even if it was a week, it would all be for nothing. How could he leave after he'd turned our family upside down to pursue his vision, with hope of offering us a secure future in case the insurance agency didn't work out? He became obsessed with success and financial stability—anything but going back to being broke and back in my parents' house, living like mice. His biggest fear was not keeping his promise of giving us the best life possible, the promise he'd made on Christmas Eve 2008.

The pressure he put on himself was debilitating, and suddenly, the once-delicious vision of having money came crashing down and became appalling. As he talked to me, he began to realize that happiness and money were not as closely related as he once thought. You can make money and still find a way to enjoy making memories with family. He was confused and frustrated by the realization that he'd worked his ass off to have the life he dreamed of, only to have no life at all. While he was looking for happiness outside, we were home, waiting for him, waiting to hug him, love him, and make him smile. He kept telling me that I'd created this "monster" because of my desire for a better life. I then realized that his definition of a better life was accumulating enormous amounts of money, but mine was having a good amount of money for peace of mind so that we could enjoy life. We could have it all; we could build a successful company and successful relationships with those we loved. I began to realize that James was battling a similar war that I was battling. His desire for financial success was always fighting his desire for joy and family time. My desire for wanting to give my all to my family was fighting my desire for wanting to do something for myself on a deeply personal level.

It was all about balance, something of which both of us had zero understanding. I was obsessed with building a happy life for Milana, and he was obsessed with building a company that would make for a happy life for us.

I understood that he needed to work hard and then reap the benefits, but if the goal was to make money, we would never reap the benefits, as he could never make enough, and it would become a sickness. The goal was to balance making money and enjoying it at the same time. We didn't need this life he thought he was building for us. I didn't need the nice house, nice car, and fancy clothing, not at the cost of watching the person Milana and I loved so much come home in complete agony. Milana didn't need the luxuries; she needed a dad. I didn't need pricey material possessions; I needed my best friend at home to share my joys and sorrows. No adult ever grows up and says, "My dad was never around and was angry all the time, but I had a shit load of toys that more than made up for it."

On that balcony, our marriage took a huge shift. We were able to finally share our deepest, darkest thoughts. I realized the gift of enormous problems and the curse of little ones. It was the big problems that forced us to speak and express what was on our minds. Little problems weren't important enough to talk about or to disturb the peace, but they added up, never really leaving because they were never resolved. Just because we didn't feel like bringing up a little problem or making a big deal out of it didn't mean it wouldn't resurface. It seemed like so many times I would smile through the pain so that I could create a peaceful home, only to have a massive blowout that would take days for us and Milana to recover.

We had such an amazing connection on that balcony. My heart broke for James, and I felt my body melt after months of pent-up frustration. We made a promise to each other to make enjoying life together our number-one goal, even if it was just to take a walk or share a hug. James made the decision to leave the academy, days before graduation. He couldn't stand another day, and I supported him.

We booked a vacation to Mexico that very night and never looked back on the nine months of hell we'd gone through. Life was simply too good to allow for resentment or bad feelings, many of which were resolved. The day after we came back from Mexico, Milana and I began going to the most beautiful beach club on the Jersey Shore. The owner of our townhome also owned the club and offered us a free membership that was valued at $36,000 a summer. The palm trees, the white sand, the pool, the ocean—everything was there to make me feel like I was experiencing heaven on earth.

It was across the street from our house, and we spent our days there, basking in bliss together as a family.

My entire emotional being changed, a beautiful outcome of addressing problems and feeling the freedom to say what was in my heart. I felt as if I was rewired somehow to view the relationships with myself, my husband, and the world differently. Instead of running from my pain, I faced it. Instead of running from our marital strife, I faced it. Instead of shushing the voice in my heart, I faced it. I faced everything head-on, with an open heart and an attentive ear. I realized that it was a lot less painful to face my problems than it was to suppress them and have them nagging at me on a daily basis. You can either beat around the bush as you slowly scratch yourself or jump in, feel the thorns, and begin to heal. Though I hadn't mastered this skill completely, I was at least trying. The energy running through my body was empowering. It was super-charged with positivity, and I felt as if I changed the dimensions of my world. I felt as if what was before my eyes had been invisible for years.

I realized that during our most trying times, James would often shut me out in hopes of protecting his inner thoughts and feelings. I was too closed off from the world myself and plagued by my own guilt of not sharing my inner thoughts. Just as his face would often display unhappiness and irritability, my face would display a smile, masking unhappiness and irritability. I feared asking him what was wrong because I feared he would ask me the same thing. I couldn't let my guard down for fear of being imperfect or weak, and it was that thought that caged me in my own world. Once I stopped lying to myself, my family, and the world and told the truth, I felt more free.

On one perfect summer evening, I took a deep breath and told James, "I don't want to stay home with Milana anymore. I want to put her in daycare and work with you, like we always did. I miss being Bonnie and Clyde."

I was going against everything I preached. I would sneer at women who let daycare raise their kids. I even lost respect for and friendships with women who chose to work outside the home instead of cooking, cleaning, and tending to their children. I judged with anger and frustration because, truthfully, I was jealous of them. I too wanted to pee alone—how lucky they were! They got to spend their days doing what they wanted to do. They were progressing in life and finding ways to balance motherhood, their own desires, and their marriages. I was caging myself in my own home, thinking my absolute devotion and borderline obsessive control over raising Milana was because I was too scared to face myself. It was easier to care for someone else; it was hard to care for myself because it would have required an enormous amount of soul searching. It's easier to put the dishes in the dishwasher, do a load of laundry, and make lunch than to look in the mirror and ask myself, "Who am I and why am I here? What am I going to contribute to the world that will make an impact?" What I wanted to truly do was so far from my reach I just shushed my voice--and I did so for three years.

In totally synchronicity with the year, as soon as I had a thought or desire, somehow the universe would rearrange itself to serve me. In August I found an amazing daycare for Milana, and (to my dismay) she loved every minute of it. I was so happy because her experience there gave her so much more than I ever could give. I let my little girl go. I let controlling her go, and it felt so liberating. I chose to continue nursing her on demand. I couldn't imagine her surviving without my boobs. I always envisioned my breasts as machine guns. With my milk, I could let Milana go anywhere, and no matter what germs she picked up, I could destroy them with a little bit of breast milk. I never worried about her getting sick. I knew that between her immune system and my amazing milk, she could easily overcome anything. Making milk was my "super power," and I loved the empowering feeling it gave me.

One day, when Milana was almost two years old and had been in daycare about a week, we were enjoying a ride through the grocery store. She was her usual smiling, laughing self, and I adored her. Then, at the checkout, my perfectly happy little love's head spun 360 degrees, and some sort of monster appeared before me. She began to yell and scream, wanting to get out of the cart. I let her down, and she began to kick me, screaming as she lay on the floor of the store. *Oh, my God! What is happening?* I thought. *Is this the terrible-twos temper tantrums I've heard of? What is happening to my child?* I was so angry about her losing control that it made her tantrum escalate even more.

Luckily, a very nice lady came by and said, "Don't worry about anyone here. We are all rooting for you and are sympathizing. No one here is judging you, so calm down, and let her finish blowing off steam."

Her words made me realize that my anger was more related to my looking like a horrible mother than focusing on how Milana was feeling. As I stood there, speechless, watching her scream and cry, I remembered how many times throughout the day I wished I could do that and how beneficial it would be to let off some steam every now and then. Suddenly, I felt so much compassion for her. I was able to somehow understand her desire to let off steam after a long, tiring day.

I went back to the day when I'd had my own temper tantrum and lost control on Christmas Eve. On that day, I was punching James and screaming at the top of my lungs, losing all desire to control myself. It was an urge to let go and release all my emotions. Even though Milana's emotional need to let loose on the floor was not fueled by pent-up frustration, I somehow understood where she was coming from. I thought about what I would have wanted from James when I was having a meltdown. Ah yes. I would have wanted him to sit beside me and let me do my thing. Don't ask me to stop; don't ask me to calm down; and don't say a word, just compassionately watch me.

I sat on the floor next to Milana and said, "I totally understand where you're coming from. A few hours ago at the mall, I wanted to do the same thing, just scream right there on the floor in the middle of the store. You can finish doing your thing. I'm right here when you're ready for a hug."

As I sat beside her, I didn't care what anyone thought of us. All I cared about was allowing her to finish. Within a few minutes, she was done. I picked her up and hugged her. We were both in shock over what had happened. This new expression of emotion was as new to her as it was to me.

When I finished paying for our groceries and we got in the car, I sat with her for a few minutes.

"Milana, what happened back there?"

"I tire, Mommy," she said in a sorry voice.

Aha, being tired is one trigger that can set off a meltdown; I needed to watch for that. At home, she would nap whenever she felt tired, but in daycare, there was a set time for naps, and it was all new to her. That night, as she lay sleeping in my arms as she always did, I did some research online about meltdowns. I wanted so badly to understand why kids have tantrums that are so severe and violent. I learned that it's due to their lacking the words to express their emotions. Teaching kids words to express their emotions is the first step in helping them put a name on what they are feeling. Words, such as sad and angry, can really help a child express an emotion.

I also learned that being mindful of the child's needs helps tremendously. A few days later, I was lucky enough to watch another episode of her mid-mall tantrum, but this time I was ready. We had been shopping for fall clothing all afternoon, and I saw her face display signs of a meltdown. I was praying for her to hold off for a few more minutes so that I could finish paying and get out of the store. Unfortunately, she didn't want to wait and began to cry. Then the cry got louder, and she decided that the floor was the best place to "express herself."

I took a few deep breaths and leaned in to tell her in her ear, "Milana, you have been so patient with me all day, and I thank you for that. I can imagine how you feel. Honestly, I want to lie right next to you and cry myself. You can have your meltdown for thirty seconds and cry all you want, but then I need you to be back to your amazing self. Deal?"

She thought it was funny that I wanted to lie next to her, and no matter how hard she tried, she just couldn't proceed with crying. She still lay there for a few minutes, but it was from sheer exhaustion, not because she was frustrated. I was okay with that and was relieved that a little sense of humor got me through what could have been another epic meltdown. The more I watched for signs of her behavior, the more prepared I was to handle situations before they escalated. I felt so close to her that I could feel her mood swings well before they become full-blown crying fits.

James decided to take control of his life, eliminating anything that would contribute to his frustration. He decided to part ways with his business partner, leaving the position that initially was mine open for me again. It was the perfect opportunity for me to go back to work and feel like a human being again— as in, doing my hair and makeup and finally getting out of the yoga pants I'd lived in for two years. James and I had a blast working together—he felt like he wasn't alone, and I felt productive. I got to know many of our clients and would help James with whatever he needed. It brought us closer together; we were in sync, always talking about work and celebrating every major client. One of the greatest aspects of working together was having a deeper understanding of each other's day-to-day stresses and struggles. When I was home, I didn't know why James would sometimes come home grumpy or irritated. I was just annoyed by his lack of excitement to see us. Now, I was there to witness some of the stresses and heartache he experienced when losing a client or not getting a deal done. I felt more compassion toward him when he was down, and it brought us closer with each passing day. Our roles began to shift as well. It was no longer my job to "tend to the house" and his job to "make money."

We were doing things together now. He would make dinner, and I would clean up; he would throw in a load of laundry, and we would talk while folding the clothes. The atmosphere in our house became so light and airy. Milana began to open up and give James a chance to bond with her, to share stories and to play tickle monster with her. Every time we were all together, we felt to so free and open, having plenty of time during the day to talk, but more important, we truly enjoyed Milana. When we smiled, we truly smiled—not to cover up tears. When we laughed, we didn't stop until at least one of us peed our pants. When we would go to the park, we played until the sun went down.

The force that brought so much joy to our lives was getting stronger and stronger. That force, I now understand, was my exhilarating feeling of freedom. I loved missing Milana when she was in daycare; it was a great feeling that I'd never experienced. It made me appreciate her more and made me more patient with her. I was a better, more energetic mother because of the time spent apart. The more love James and I gave each other, the less we felt the need to judge or fear being judged by each other. The more we understood each other, the kinder we were, and powerful, positive emotions forced the world around us to be of service to us.

In October, we celebrated Milana's second birthday by throwing a beautiful (some say over-the-top) party. Something profound happened within me during that party. I was standing by the dance floor, watching Milana hop up and down with Elmo and Mickey, and suddenly, as if in slow motion, I saw her enormous smile and her eyes that twinkled with joy. Her pigtails flopped up and down, and she exuded genuine joy. She was so grateful that everyone was there. She was so happy that we were celebrating her. I couldn't help the tears that rolled down my face. I felt such a deep love and appreciation for Milana, as if I was falling in love with her for the very first time. During this moment in my life, I was able to finally feel what I had struggled to feel since I closed off my emotions after losing Juliana. It was so liberating to finally experience the love I wanted so badly to feel when Milana was born. I felt such enormous gratitude to James for giving us a life where we could provide magical moments like these. He came up to me as I watched her and pulled me close to him. His eyes teared up too. He'd done it; he'd given us the life he promised he would. I thought that was the best of life, but I had no idea where life was about to take us next.

Money kept flowing in, and by December we decided it was time to buy a home we could grow in. We wanted a backyard, grass, and more of a family-oriented community. Sea Bright was an awesome place to party but not to raise a family. Our search often led us to homes that had major problems. The cycle kept repeating itself. We would find a home, accept that there were certain things it lacked, make an offer—and the home would be sold to someone else before our offer was presented to the owners. After losing three homes, we began to lose excitement. But as our angel Juliana would have it, a miracle was about to happen.

A few days before Christmas, the home we were absolutely in love with went off the market. Minutes later, we got a notification that a new house in our price range was available. We looked at the pictures and almost fell off our chairs. We put on our shoes (we liked to feel at home at the office), put the remainder of our lunch back in the fridge, and peeled out of the parking lot, racing to go see the house.

We entered the community and, with eyes wide open, both whispered under our breath, "Wow." The homes were traditional colonial style with manicured lawns and playgrounds in almost every backyard—that was my favorite aspect since there would be plenty of kids for Milana to play with. On one side of the sidewalk, a young mother was enjoying a walk with her baby in the stroller. On the other side, a group of women my age were jogging. There was so much life here in this community. I couldn't wait to see the house we'd found online. After looking carefully at house numbers, we finally pulled up to number 11. We couldn't believe how magnificent the home was—all brick with large windows, standing gracefully up on a hill. I asked James to double-check the house number because we hadn't seen any homes like this in our price range.

"Babe, this is it; this is the right house," James said as he left the car so excited he didn't even bother closing his door. Standing on the sidewalk in awe, James called our agent and begged to get us in as soon as possible.

Our agent called early on New Year's Eve morning to let us know we could see the house. As I do every year, I went for a walk. It had been a wonderful year. What started out as a journey to find my voice and then to have the courage to share it had helped me find who I was—as well as who James was. How far our marriage had come! We'd gone from sharing a house like roommates, to seriously considering divorce, to sharing our deepest pain, to working together in every aspect of our lives. Our home went from being a place that caged me to a place where I felt most free. I was in an amazing place in life, and the energy around me made me feel like I could fly. It wasn't that major changes happened within the people around me; no, the biggest change was my perception of what I was worthy of experiencing and my having the balls to ask for that which I wanted.

Then something amazing happened. I realized that the house I'd envisioned on this very day two years prior was the exact brick, central colonial we were going to see later that day. Even the double front doors, where I saw myself standing, holding a baby and two girls holding my dress, was identical. Every detail of that vision was exactly the house and the community. Even the spiral staircase I got glimpse of as I stood in the doorway was the same. How could it be that the place where I'd escape during my lonely, painful nights was actually now my possible reality? I was in disbelief that this had happened to me for the second time. My heart was pounding; I started to walk so fast I was almost running. *Oh, my God*, I thought. *Is this really happening? Is my vision really coming true?* I began to run, and tears were streaming down my cheeks. It was cold outside, but my body felt warm. I finally understood the power of visualization, of dreaming and believing I was meant for so much more.

I felt Juliana running with me, smiling at me as I always thought she did when I had the epiphanies she so beautifully orchestrated. I felt like screaming to the world, *"Thank you, thank you, thank you!"* What a journey it had been. I felt joy and gratitude in every cell of my body.

My vision for the year ahead, 2012, involved having another baby. Milana demanded a lot from me, and I didn't feel I was ready for another child until she went to daycare—and I got to use the bathroom by myself. I thought how wonderful it would be to finally get pregnant without worrying about money or where we would put the baby or if we could handle it emotionally. I came home and gave James and Milana the biggest hug. I felt so much joy in my heart as I got dressed to go see the inside of the house we had been dreaming about—the house I knew deep down inside was already ours.

When we walked inside, we were both in speechless awe. The layout for the massive five-bedroom, four-bath home was absolutely perfect, and the backyard looked like something out of a magazine. As we walked around, we felt as if we were home. Milana was comfortable running between the two massive staircases and chose which of the bedrooms was hers. I already saw what I wanted to change and how we would arrange the furniture. James saw how he was going to turn the backyard into a piece of heaven. There was no need to look any further; the home was ours. We gave an offer on the house on January 2, 2012, and then braced ourselves, as we'd taken a big chance by low-balling. I was so grateful for all the other home offers that had fallen through, and I believed with all my heart that Juliana had brought us there. The next series of events confirmed my belief in miracles. It felt like the tides had changed, and wave after wave of miracles began to flood our life on a daily basis. The beginning of 2012 was a very happy time for our family, full of hope and amazing things to come.

One freezing January morning, however, I couldn't lift my head off the pillow. I felt unusually tired and nauseated. As I nursed Milana, I felt sore and didn't want her near my breasts. My first thought was, *Oh shit*, but my next thought was, *Wow, that was a quick manifestation of my desire.* Just four days earlier, I'd had my first itch for a baby. A few hours later, a home pregnancy test confirmed that I was pregnant! James and I were happy but had an underlying feeling of guilt because Milana was our everything. We were obsessively in love with her. How could we share that love with another baby? Those thoughts quickly disappeared when we told Milana we were going to have a baby. She was so excited that she spent the next few weeks tending to all her dolls, showing us that she was ready to help out with the baby.

A few weeks later, on February 14, James sent me a text that read: "Want to be my valentine?" I laughed, reading it. "Yes!" I yelled out toward his office, which was about six feet away from my desk. We decided to go to Red Bank, a little town filled with many hip restaurants. The food and service was horrible though entertaining, since we couldn't stop laughing as we poked and played with the food as it came out.

After lunch, I started to feel cramping but thought it was just the baby growing, so I kept quiet about the pain. Toward evening, the pain got more intense, and I started to spot blood. I knew something was wrong, and WebMD confirmed it. I excused myself from dinner and went upstairs to lie down, but the pain intensified. I took an Advil PM and finally fell asleep. I woke up at sunrise to the most beautiful little voice singing, "Happy bir'day to you, happy bir'day to you, Mama." I still had my eyes closed, drowning in the bliss, feeling her love as she moved the hair off my face and kissed my eyes. I couldn't stop smiling. This was a beautiful way to begin my birthday. *What an extraordinary gift she is to me*, I thought. She put her head on my chest, and I inhaled her sweet scent and caressed her soft hair. Then, that perfect moment ended abruptly when I felt something wet. I got up to go to the bathroom and saw that I had miscarried the baby. Deep inside I'd known the pregnancy had not been progressing for days because all my symptoms disappeared overnight, but I'd hoped this was just an easy pregnancy, not the end of one.

I spent the day at home in bed, thinking back to my twenty-fifth birthday and of the incredible sadness I'd felt because of my dying daughter. I'd been through a lot, but I also realized that without these heartbreaking moments, I could not have fully enjoyed the blissful moments. I made peace with this most recent loss, took a deep breath, and began to pray for my next pregnancy.

At this point in my life, dodging hits was a part of life I'd mastered. I felt so strong as a person and found peace in thinking that I had a new angel to watch over me. It was a very inspiring and uplifting thought. Maybe Juliana needed help from another angel; maybe this was all for the purpose of helping me.

A few days later at the office, the phone rang as we were having lunch. I almost fell off the chair from laughing at James as he tried to quickly chew and swallow the egg-and-cheese croissant he was eating. "James Nelligan," he said through the food in his cheeks. "How can I help you?"

His face changed as he listened to the caller. He stared right in to my eyes, not saying a word. I didn't know if something terrible had happened, as his face was frozen and his eyes wide open.

"Got it, yup, okay, thank you," he said and then hung up the phone. He turned to me. "Kat, we got the house and so much more."

We'd heard that short sales, which is how our dream house was listed, can take up to two years to finalize. It had been only two months, and we had a move-in date! The next series of events confirmed my belief in my mantra: what's meant to be will be, regardless of what it takes. On January 1, President Obama had asked banks to accept offers on homes that were close to going into foreclosure. In our particular situation, the current homeowners had taken out an enormous home equity line of credit on the house when the market was at its peak, and the buyer was responsible for paying it off. The house had been on the market for two years and had many price reductions, but no one wanted to take on the other people's debt—so the house was patiently waiting for us!

By the time we gave our offer of almost $80,000 below asking price, the owners apparently had a change of heart. Not only did they accept our offer, selling the house for half its value, but they also paid our attorney fees and closing costs and for a moving company to pack and unpack us.

I realized then that the biggest difference between lucky people and unlucky people is that lucky people believe they are lucky, and unlucky people believe they are unlucky. That's all there is to it. As we became more and more grateful, seeing magic all around us and making all our dreams become a reality, we increased our energy. I call it moving between worlds; the world we used to live in was filled with difficult circumstances and painful occurrences, and we lacked luck. It was often cloudy, and every positive opportunity fell through, sucking at the wind beneath our wings. But now, our days were filled with lots of sunshine, and even when it rained, it smelled good and sounded relaxing. Now, we realized that we tipped the scale of our life and leaned to the positive side.

When bad things happened, we felt bad and had negative thoughts, which attracted more negative circumstances, more negative thoughts, and more bad feelings, and thus attracting more reasons to stay low. I finally understood the meaning of "when it rains, it pours." I wanted to use that saying to my advantage and let the rains of amazing circumstances pour as a never-ending stream of reasons to smile and celebrate.

Chapter 7

We spent our fifth wedding anniversary in our new home, drinking champagne and unpacking the last of the boxes. James was so proud and happy to move us into this dream house. I kept toasting him and thanking him for keeping his promises. He had done everything I'd asked of him on that Christmas night in 2008. We were now living in a home enormous enough to house as many children as we wanted, a house that could be the meeting place for all our friends and family. As we sat outside on the steps—no patio furniture yet—passing the bottle of champagne back and forth between us, James started kissing me. He whispered, "Happy anniversary, babe. Hope you like your gift."

A few weeks later, Milana began going through a phase where she was constantly preparing for a sibling. "This seat next to me is for my baby brother. Mommy is having a baby." And often during dinner, she would leave food on her plate and say, "This is for the baby in Mommy's belly. I'm going to leave this for him."

James and I didn't think anything of it; we just assumed it was a phase she was going through. A few days later, as we were painting Milana's playroom, James looked at me as I rolled paint on the wall and said, "Wait ... lift your arms up again."

As I did, I looked down at my stomach. It was bulging out of my shorts, and the button was straining to stay closed. I had been feeling a bit tired lately but I thought it was because of all the work we were doing in the house. Luckily, just the night before I had unpacked a pregnancy test. I'd heard the saying, "new house, new baby," and I'd like to confirm that it is very true. Amazingly, when I went to the doctor a few days later, he told me that I conceived right around April 24, our first night in the house. Our third baby was conceived with so much love—and so much champagne. It was truly a bubbly love child.

We spent the summer enjoying the pool and watching Milana learn how to not drown (what she was doing wouldn't really be considered swimming). I thought that life at home just couldn't get any better … but life outside home needed some readjusting.

James hired a new employee who would handle my workload so that I could pursue an opportunity to work for an energy company. I was really excited to learn and work for an industry outside of insurance, but when I began working, I realized that I didn't want to change careers. I just wanted to not do insurance! Even though I was miserable, I was still somehow number one, beating every record I set and praised on a daily basis. But no matter how much money I made or how well I did, something inside me was always nagging. I felt like there was so much more to me than going door to door, offering a reduced electricity rate to business owners.

I loved getting dressed up and having somewhere to go—anything but stay home—but I found no joy in what I was doing. The one thought that kept running through my mind was that I had every attribute to have an amazing career I loved, so why couldn't I figure it out? Why couldn't I find my purpose in life? Why would God instill so much in me but not show me the purpose of my life? The truth is, I denied myself the soul search because I wanted so badly to be a good mother and wife. I wanted to work solely as an excuse to keep Milana in daycare and so I could wear all the beautiful dresses I'd accumulated. I felt independent when I made money, and that was an important feeling for me to have. My vision of myself was that I could clean a massive 5,000-square-foot house, cook up a three-course meal fresh every day, and still tend to the children 100 percent. I wanted to be supermom, and honestly, it was easier to tend to my duties for others than it was to face my burning desire to be someone who could influence the world and share my voice. Same recurring problem, year after year, with no idea how I was going to finally figure it all out.

I woke up in the middle of the night, thinking about what I would do when the kids got older. What career would I chose for myself when I could no longer hide behind my duties of tending to the children. Up to this point, every job opportunity had fallen into my lap, and I'd just run with it, never really thinking about what I wanted to do. I was good at sales, but being good at something was not enough to satisfy me. I accepted any job that didn't require my presence at an office and gave me freedom to choose my own hours— as long as I was still able to put my mothering and housekeeping duties first. I lived with the consequences of shushing my inner voice, which asked me on a daily basis to explore my dreams. I suffered with anxiety that nagged at me but not enough to compel me to look deeper into the problem. What was I going to do? I was pregnant; how could I begin a new career? I had responsibilities to my family. How could I abandon my baby to selfishly build a dream for myself? I convinced myself that working at my current job in energy sales was where I should stay, even if it wasn't my "calling." The timing wasn't right, and I wasn't ready.

One hot July day I returned for the third time to see a client, as his company's name continued to be misspelled on the contract. James gave me a ride because I was too nauseated and sick to drive. I was in such a state of depression. I hated every second of working the job I had. My body felt weak; my gut was telling me to leave this job and never return.

I walked in to see Mr. Jones, and he looked at me with compassionate eyes. "Katerina, the name of my company is spelled wrong," he said. "I am not going to go through this a fourth time, and I suggest you don't either."

My commission was seventy dollars. What the fuck was I doing?

Was my desire to get out of the house and feel productive that strong? I walked out, threw the contract on the hood of James's car, and put my head down on the windshield. I was done. I couldn't even talk.

James got out of the car and hugged me as he whispered, "I'm sorry, Kat."

Then I said, "Let's get the fuck out of town, I want to drive for a really long time. I need to think about what I'm doing. What have I done in my life that I feel like I don't deserve to enjoy summer and life? Why is everything a struggle when I try to work?"

I had a craving to go to Bar Harbor, Maine. I had been there many years earlier, and I wanted the awe-inspiring energy of that place. Practicing my "do and say what you really want," I blurted out, "I want to go to Bar Harbor."

James helped me in the car and looked at me with eyes that said he was willing to do anything to cheer me up. "Then that's where were going."

We went home, quickly packed, picked up Milana from daycare, and began our sixteen-hour journey. We didn't talk much; I had a lot of thinking to do. Milana, luckily, was so tired that she slept most of the way. I thought about how I keep screwing myself, over and over, paralyzing myself with my own rules. I wanted to find out why I was attached to the idea of working. Why did I think working would bring me pleasure and make me feel productive when it was doing everything but that? Why couldn't I just leave? What was keeping me at my job? Was it my fear of being a stay-at-home mom again, a label that sent shivers down my spine?

I reached out to Juliana, asking her for an epiphany and a change in my thinking. The further I got out of my head, the closer I got to God and to my soul. Everyone loved me at home; everyone thought I was enough. Why didn't I think this way? Caring for my family and being an amazing mother was a huge role and a very productive one too. Making a beautiful, warm, clean home filled with laughter, fun, and delicious meals shared together was my being productive at its best. I contributed to the family, even if it wasn't a financial contribution. I finally let go of the idea that productivity and contribution go hand in hand with money—at least I let it go a little bit. Amazingly, when I began to share these thoughts with James, he said he wouldn't think less of me if I wasn't working. His biggest reason for wanting me to work was because I seemed happy getting out, and he loved seeing me crush it in sales. No one was happy when I was depressed, and I wanted everyone to be happy. I had to break free from my own mental cage. I decided to never go back to that job again. In that moment, I looked out the window and saw an entirely new world. The trees were so green and the grass was so lush, and the sun was pleasantly blinding.

The most magnificent sunrise greeted us by the time we arrived at the hotel. I again felt magic all around me, and the universe gave me plenty of reasons to smile. It was that change in energy that I craved so badly. Thank God that I spoke up about my desire to get away.

The first night in our room I smelled something awful. (Being pregnant, I had the nose of a well-trained dog.) I went to the front desk in hopes of changing our room, and a woman there greeted me with a huge smile. I guess she felt my renewed energy. I told her that the room smelled, and I couldn't deal with it because of my condition.

She smiled and said, "I am so sorry. We have a suite that overlooks the ocean. Would you like me to send someone to move your things?"

Not only did we get a room in the hotel (the same hotel where President Obama has vacationed), but we got it for the price of a low-end room during their peak week of the year. Amazing things happen when you shift your energy. Suddenly, everything works out better than you could have anticipated. I tipped the scale once more toward the positive side and triggered the gates of goodness to open, flooding my life once more with reasons to feel excited about my life.

Our time in Maine was perfect in every way. More important, for me, the ice cream was phenomenal, and our little vacation brought us even closer together. Once we returned home, I didn't go back to work, but I didn't quit. I liked my boss, and we had many talks about where the company was going. Those talks qualified me as an employee—or so I thought. When I was finally invited for my monthly review, I had nothing to show them, and so they had to let me go. Being fired on the week when I qualified for unemployment was another God-sent gift, and I received checks during a time in my pregnancy when I was simply immobile.

James found a company that was looking for a licensed professional to explain health insurance to seniors. It was a rewarding opportunity; we stayed home and called senior citizens to explain their benefits to them. The money was paid to our company, so I still qualified for unemployment. Lucky breaks were pouring in. I truly believe if I hadn't freed myself from my own mentality of working hard for money so that I could feel productive, I would still be in a massively deep hole of a depression. Instead, I was home, enjoying my pregnancy, caring for the house, shopping, cooking, and being an amazing mother, all while contributing financially.

Sometimes, the first step is moving past our own thoughts, and once we do that, the universe somehow rearranges itself in such a way that we are left with little choice but to believe in the powers that be. I saw an image on Facebook that showed a horse tied to a plastic chair, but she thought she was tied to a post. Sometimes we think we are held down to a massive post, but often it's just a tiny plastic chair that can be moved with little effort. The cages we build for ourselves are often made of gingerbread, not steel. We can bite our way through the walls—and enjoy a snack too!

Our first Christmas in our new home was absolutely magical. We were bursting with joy, gratitude, and enormous hope for the New Year. The day after Christmas, Milana and I were playing with all her new toys and gearing up for a huge snowstorm that was supposed to be "epic," as the newsman put it.

James called me and said, "Pack us up. We're going to a warm place. Our flight is in six hours."

He hung up before I could tell him that because I was thirty-six weeks pregnant, I most likely wouldn't be allowed on the plane. I packed anyway and couldn't think of a better way to weather the storm. I did get a lot of frightened stares from the passengers on the plane as my belly and I made our way down the aisle. I assured everyone my previous labors had been long, so they had nothing to worry about.

"Don't worry," I told the flight attendant. "I'm just really bloated."

We arrived in Florida in the middle of the night. When the cab driver pulled up to the Ritz-Carlton, my mouth dropped and I looked at James with disbelief. He hugged Milana and me and said, "Merry Christmas, my loves." All the visions that I'd lived through in my head during the most devastating years of my life were now my reality. The life I'd envisioned was now where I lived, and it was even better than I'd dreamed. I felt so close to God, Juliana, and heaven on earth. I felt strong, as if I could do anything as long as I had my higher self by my side.

After failing to progress with my last two pregnancies, I wanted to learn everything I could about giving birth vaginally after two C-sections. I'd felt such sadness and a sense of failure after the last two attempts to have a natural vaginal birth. I felt broken. It was my dream to give birth and feel the baby pass through my body. I was in awe of how beautiful women were during labor. No matter how weak they appeared in life, during labor they looked heroic to me. My deepest desire to give birth on my own propelled me in to doing massive amounts of research on how to successfully VBAC. I wasn't looking for medical data; I wanted stories from real women who defied the odds. I was in a place in life where I defied odds on a daily basis. I wasn't afraid of statistics or numbers. I found a woman on YouTube through ICAN (International Cesarean Awareness Network), who'd had a vaginal delivery after four C-sections. I was so inspired by her story. She too had struggled with feeling broken. I felt like I wasn't alone. I also came across a few women online who were the wind beneath my wings; they had no doubt that I could do it.

My obsession with reading about birth and the mental connection we have with our bodies consumed me. What I found was absolutely life-changing for me and empowered me like never before. I went on daily walks and did my affirmations: "My body is perfect. It will open up and birth my baby. It's designed perfectly. I will give birth through me. I will get through the pain. I will not fear. I am designed for this. But if my body doesn't comply, I will still love it and be grateful to it for giving me a precious gift. I will forgive myself. I am perfect, regardless of how I give birth."

I was so in tune with my body and my baby. I envisioned pushing and my body opening up to deliver a baby—there was no doubt in my mind. I was ready to give myself all the time I needed to dilate, always making sure we were safe. As deep as my desire was to deliver without intervention, my desire for the safety of my baby and myself was just as deep. James was my rock. He had no doubt I could do this, and I credit his support for the events that transpired next.

Thursday, January 17, was my due date. I woke up feeling energized and excited, with a craving for a long, fast power-walk. Since it was two degrees outside, the mall was my only option. I walked and walked, and then I took another long walk, followed by more walking. After another walk, I still felt as if I'd drunk an enormous amount of caffeine. I decided to walk up and down the massive staircase in the center of the mall, over and over again. After four hours of walking the mall, I thought I heard my shoe rip and decided to go home.

After dinner, I went upstairs to snuggle with Milana. We fell asleep together in the comfortable position of her acting as my "body pillow," her favorite. I fell asleep as I always did, holding hands with her. Around 11:00 p.m., I woke up because the pain in my abdomen made me squeeze Milana's hand so hard that she slightly woke up. My first contraction was less than an hour before the end of the day on my due date—how textbook of me! I spent the next few hours on my hands and knees but still in bed, riding the pain. Milana was right there with me, rubbing my back and kissing me as my breathing got deeper. I held her hand, squeezing it through every contraction, but no matter how hard I squeezed, she never showed discomfort. I was laboring with my three-year-old as my birth coach! She brought me water; she rubbed my back; she was my savior.

I kept calling the doctor to tell her my progress, but she told me that the contractions were still too far apart for me to go to the hospital. James was busy finishing up the crown molding in Milana's room and would check on me throughout the night. Finally, around 3:00 a.m., I was concerned that Milana had been up with me and decided to go downstairs so she could sleep.

Being alone in our dark living room, lit only by the moonlight shining through the window, was comforting. The couch was my favorite place in the house, and I felt free to make scary, loud noises as I got through the pain with each contraction. I was so in tune with myself and was grateful for every contraction, no matter how painful it was. *This is it*, I kept thinking. *I am finally experiencing what I dreamed about for all these months and all these years.*

As the sun began to rise, my contractions subsided and ultimately stopped completely. I fell asleep, and when I woke up a few hours later, I felt as if I hadn't labored at all. I felt energized, hungry, and happy. James made me call the doctor to tell her how close my contractions had been the night before—a consistent every five minutes for five hours. I didn't want anyone to know when my early labor had begun for fear they would start the clock on how much time I had to dilate before insisting I needed a C-section.

On Friday, January 18, around noon, my contractions picked up again with the same intensity but at longer intervals. I told my doctor, and she asked us to meet her at the hospital to check on the baby and my progress. We arrived a few hours later and were greeted by a kind and wonderful nurse, who assured us the baby was great and that laboring for a few days was normal. She told me that she labored for four days, on and off. Her story made me feel really confident in my body. We went home, having found peace in knowing that everything was perfect with our baby. We asked my mom to come over for support and to help out with Milana, just in case I went into active labor that night.

I spent the evening contracting on and off, moaning and panting. I belly-danced, swaying my hips left to right to alleviate the pain, and it worked wonders. My bladder and uterus had grown together because of the excess scar tissue from the previous C-sections. Every time I contracted, the pain was excruciating, as I felt my organs tear apart. At one point I told James I wanted to go for a walk outside.

"Your screaming and moaning will scare the kids building a snowman outside," he responded. "It's better you stay indoors, away from the public."

I agreed; no need to scare the children. Interestingly, Milana was not fazed at all by my crying and belly dancing during each contraction. She calmly fed me potato chips and water—that was her comfort food, so she must have thought it should help me too. At 10:00 p.m., I went to bed, feeling exhausted from panting and dancing all day. Plus, the contractions at that point had completely stopped for more than an hour. I slept all night snuggled up next to Milana. When I woke up, I was face-to-face with my girl. I could feel the warmth of her breath, and I thought of how amazing our journey had been with her as my one and only. For the last three years, every single night I went to sleep with her face as the last thing I saw before my eyes closed and the first thing I saw when I awoke. I felt a little guilty that she would have to move over and make space for a new baby; she'd have to be more independent as I cared for another little gift.

My intuition kicked in, and I realized this might be the last morning we'd wake up together as a family of three. I moved the hair off Milana's face and stared at her perfection, her incredibly peaceful state. I basked in the last few moments of it being just us. I spooned her, holding her close, as I lost myself in the euphoria I felt whenever I was with her. I was so grateful for the amazing privilege of being her mother. This amazing three-year-old had the deepest, oldest, most beautiful soul I had ever met.

I spent Saturday, January 19, doing laundry, as my nesting instinct kicked into full gear. Everyone was happy to have their socks folded perfectly (for the first time, I think). My contractions came and went, but this time I felt them much stronger. I had been taking red raspberry tea leaf pills to help tone my uterus in the last four weeks of my pregnancy. These vitamins make contractions very strong and productive but not necessarily close together. I kept belly dancing and going up and down the stairs throughout most of the day. I don't know why, but going up the stairs felt so good to me. The belly dancing was the only relief I felt during contractions. As I raised my hands up to the sky, closed my eyes, and swayed my hips left to right, I felt my baby move down with each contraction. I visualized my body opening up as my baby pressed down on my cervix. We laughed a lot and tried to enjoy the unusually long labor process. I had so much respect for my body and gladly gave it all the time it needed. I felt patient and not at all anxious, as I had felt with my two previous labors. *I've waited so long for this moment*, I thought. *What's a few more days in the grand scheme of things?* Besides, I was loving the ride.

I'd never had the journey of laboring and then delivering. With Milana, I'd been pregnant, had a few contractions, and then the baby was cut out of me. With Juliana, the journey was horrific, as I was drugged beyond comprehension. The journey prepares you for the baby coming into your world. I was in awe of my body and the process of its gearing up to deliver a life. A woman's body is the only portal that brings souls from heaven to earth. This incredible privilege shouldn't be hurried. My mom took Milana to her house so that I could rest. As they were all bundled up, ready to leave, we hugged and were excited for the next time we would hug—as a family of four. Milana was already on her way out the door when she suddenly ran back to me, lifted my shirt, and kissed my belly.

"I can't wait to meet you," she said. "I love you so much, baby."

I was already very emotional, but that was the moment that brought on the waterworks! As I watched them pull out of the driveway around 6:00 p.m., it was as if my body had waited for me to be free from motherly duties. It went into full-blown labor in that exact moment. The contractions got very strong and consistent, and I knew I was getting close to active labor. I was no longer smiling and felt a shift in energy. To divert my attention from the discomfort, I watched an entire movie, but I have zero recollection of what it was about. I only know that Will Ferrell was in it. I'm a huge fan of his movies, but I know I didn't laugh even once.

At 9:00 p.m., my contractions stopped completely. I went upstairs, closed my eyes, and fell asleep instantly. I woke up with excruciating pain at midnight. I jumped out of bed and made a bath for myself. I could no longer breathe or dance through the contractions. I was now screaming every curse word I knew—and some that I made up—as the pain intensified. I wanted to be in warm water; I hoped it would give me some relief. I sat in the tub, and between contractions, all the endorphins flooded my body, drowning me in the most relaxing, euphoric feelings. I wished I could bottle the feeling; it was pure bliss. It was such a beautiful gift from my body for causing me so much pain as it contracted, pushing my baby down closer to the outside world. During contractions, I breathed and felt enormous pain, but in between, I spent my time praying. I kept thanking my body for being so magnificent and working so hard to bring a new life into the world. It was such a beautiful time in my life. I established a bond with my body that I am rewarded with to this day—the kind of bond you form when you're in the trenches during war with someone and come out alive. After the bath I felt the urge to walk around, hoping again to find some relief from the excruciating pain.

By 3:00 a.m., I had been contracting every two minutes, consistently, for three hours. Suddenly, my body transitioned to the next phase, and I contracted so hard that as I bit the mattress, my water broke. In the water I saw meconium, According to WebMD, this was a sure sign that my baby was stressed and had pooped before being born. It's a common occurrence when a baby is past the due date, even by a few days.

At 5:00 a.m., I put on my gardening sneakers and fur coat, and we headed for the hospital. I looked like a total mess (because three days isn't enough time to get ready for the hospital). I was freaking out—I never should have read anything online when I was very vulnerable and sleep-deprived.

The hospital where we were supposed to go was an hour away, but there was another one much closer. We decided to go the one nearer to our house. Panicking, we ran into the hospital, looking for Labor and Delivery and were directed to that floor. It looked like nothing short of a morgue, with blue lighting and deathly pale faces on the medical staff.

"I have been contracting for the last three days, and my water just broke, and there was meconium, and I want to have a vaginal delivery after two C-sections, so I'm going to need a room," I said in one breath between two massive contractions.

The head nurse looked at me and said in a cold voice, "We are getting you on that operating table immediately. We need to save your baby's life."

I looked at James desperately, begging for his support. It was one thing for me to try to VBAC for my own desire, but this was his child's life I was messing with as well. And the moment that made me fall in love with him deeper than ever came when he said, "They won't even give you a chance here. Let's go to the other hospital where your doctor is."

I forced a smile as I felt another massive contraction. We had two minutes before the next contraction to make it to the car, so we literally sprinted out of the hospital, taking the stairs instead of the elevator, for fear of wasting time. At this point my contractions made me curse like a sailor. We made it to the car just as I had another massive contraction. I was completely out of breath, but I called the hospital to tell them that my water broke and I saw meconium.

I expected to hear panic and dismay for my irresponsibility with regard to my child's well being, but the nurse said, "Aw, the baby made a poopie. Don't worry; it happens a lot. We are getting your room ready. See you soon." Her calm, soothing voice made me feel relaxed, peaceful, and grateful that God had put me in touch with her during the most vulnerable time of our lives

I couldn't sit upright and found comfort only when I was hugging the seat. The ride to the hospital offered my last few moments of peace—to be alone and bask in the bliss when my body was in between contractions, to pray, to relax, and to feel the baby come closer to being in arms. I loved that ride, though James later said that I screamed and begged God for mercy most of the way. Amazing that we don't remember the pain, but we remember the euphoria.

We arrived at the hospital and were greeted warmly by staff. The nurse showed us to my room, and as she opened the door to help us in, we saw the most magnificent sunrise through the window; it flooded the room with golden light. It was so uplifting that I felt my whole world light up as it prepared to welcome a new life and show support for my journey. As I was changing, a nurse came in—the same one who had comforted me a few days earlier with her story about her own four-day labor came in—and put a large jug of water on the bedside table. I was so thirsty from all the breathing; I chugged all the water almost instantly, wiped my mouth, and then was ready to labor as long as needed.

My doctor came in at seven o'clock to check me; I was five centimeters dilated. *Oh, my God*, I thought. *My body works! I can actually dilate.* All the belly dancing and visualizations of my body opening up like a flower were working! We were progressing. Even though we were on day four, we were opening up. The sun kept shining brighter, and I felt so much support from the light.

By noon I had progressed to six centimeters. It was slow, but we knew it would be, and so we respected the time my body needed to open up on its own. I felt empowered. At this point I knew progress was slow, but in the greater scheme of things, does it matter if you dilate within minutes or hours (or days)? The doctor told me that I needed an epidural so that in the event of an emergency, I could be on the operating table within minutes. I wanted so badly to feel the baby coming out. She compassionately agreed to give me a localized anesthesia, which would only numb the pain in my abdomen, allowing me to feel *everything* else.

Now that the pain was gone, I was able to focus more on meditating. I raised my energy levels by drowning my mind in thoughts of gratitude and excitement. My body began to progress much faster after the pain subsided.

I looked out the window, and the sun blinded me with its light. Somehow, the sun seems much brighter in the winter, even though the earth is farther away from it. That hospital room was filled with a warm, blissful feeling, as if all the angels had gathered to help me welcome this new life into our world. With peaceful thoughts taking over my mind, I drifted off to sleep. I woke up at five o'clock that evening to see James sleeping on the chair beside me. I felt such appreciation for him and his strength in allowing me to risk so much to fulfill my dream. As my heart flooded with love, I felt the baby move farther down. My body was perfectly doing everything it was intended to do. It's incredible what happens when we allow our bodies to take their time. When we fill them with love and appreciation, they fulfill their true potential.

The doctor came in to check on me; I was now at eight centimeters. She looked at me with her warm eyes and smiled. I was happy with the progress but didn't want to wake up James. I drifted back to sleep.

A little after six o'clock I woke up to a lot of pressure and nausea. The baby's heart rate began to speed up, and both of our oxygen levels were dropping. The doctor came in to check me and said I was almost fully dilated. *This is it*, I thought, *the moment I have waited for. It's finally happening! Time to push my baby out of my body and into the world.* All my excited feelings came to a halt, however, when

I felt the head crown. Suddenly, my desire to feel *everything* was not as wonderful as I thought it would be.

I screamed at my doctor, "Why didn't you tell me that this would hurt this bad? Why didn't any of you tell me?"

She laughed and reminded me that it would be over very soon. James woke up to my first scream, which was exaggerated and intended to get him up. He was starving and decided to get something to eat in the Labor and Delivery kitchen. By the time he got back, the doctor's bright lamp was shining directly on my "flower." I looked down and saw James devouring a box of Rice Krispies, as if he was snacking while watching a movie and not the head of his child ripping through his wife's vagina. I laughed as he shoved the rest of the contents of the box in his mouth, still chewing as he got in position to hold my leg back. I'd heard that many men are too scared to even look down there, but not my guy. He didn't even flinch.

The room filled with nurses and medical students—it wasn't very common to see a vaginal delivery after two C-sections. I didn't mind them; I even put on a special show for them by exaggerating my screaming, hoping to intimidate them (plus, I always wanted to be an actress, so that was a fun moment for me). I wanted them to see what was possible so that they would go on in their medical careers to support women who choose VBAC.

Then the show was over, and I felt the baby crown even more. I'd read about the "ring of fire" when the baby's head begins to come out. I just hadn't read about the exact level of pain it is, and I kept screaming. "This is so painful!" I said. "I am going to write a whole book on this!" I followed that by saying, "Babe, take a picture of me. I want to put this in the book."

At 6:45, I was pushing for a count of ten. I felt as if I was in another world, overwhelmed by excruciating pain. The nurses tried talking to me about the right way to position my arms and chin and how to breathe, but I felt deaf. I remembered reading that I didn't have to force the baby out; it would come out just by bringing my thoughts back to the baby. I somehow blocked the commotion happening around me. I couldn't see or hear anyone. I was one with myself, and suddenly an enormous wave of strength came over me.

"Just one more push," the doctor said in a calm, supportive voice. "The baby is almost here. Come on, Kat."

I gave one last push, and I felt the baby leave my body—it was 6:55. The doctors whisked it away to the NICU nurses. Since there was meconium in my womb, the baby had to take its first breath after having the poop suctioned out of the mouth and nose to prevent inhalation and infection. I hadn't seen the baby yet; I was still lying down with my eyes closed. I felt as if I had won gold at the Olympics. It wasn't just excitement; it was relief. I whispered, "I did it. I did it. Oh, my God, I actually did it!" A few more seconds passed, and I heard my baby cry for the first time. James and I were so relieved that it was over that we didn't even ask if it was a boy or girl.

James kept kissing my sweaty forehead and smiling with incredible joy. "You did it, babe. I am so proud of you. You did it!"

I squeezed his hand with the little bit of strength I had in me. "Thank you for letting me do this. Thank you for believing in me. Thank you for supporting me. I couldn't have done this without you."

He went over to the newborn station and then called back to me, "Babe, it's a girl! It's a baby girl."

Chapter 8

I lay back, staring at the ceiling, as the doctor began to sew me up,

"Don't put too many stitches down there," I said. "I'll be back here soon to deliver my son."

I'd thought I was having a boy this time, though I don't know why, particularly as throughout the entire pregnancy I had a recurring dream: Milana and Juliana brought me a baby swaddled in a white blanket, saying, "It's a girl, Mommy."

Then I felt such a burst of joy when I realized that the image I'd held in my mind—the image that got me through the hardest nights—was of me with a girl on each side as I held a baby boy in my arms.

The doctor finally brought me my third most magnificent gift from God. I pulled down the receiving blanket, raised her hat, and saw her beautiful face. I saw God's light right before me. She looked exactly like Juliana, so much so that both James and I were a bit taken aback. We fell so deeply in love with her that we couldn't stop smiling and crying. I felt grateful for everyone who had come forward and shared their successful VBAC stories with me. Those women had empowered me and taught me the perfection that our bodies are capable of. I was grateful for the privilege of being a mother once more, and I was overwhelmed with gratitude for being the woman who was chosen to bring this beautiful soul into the world.

I lay in my hospital room, alone with her, and my tears kept flowing. I couldn't imagine feeling a higher bliss than being with her—that is, until I came home and watched Milana meet her sister for the first time. It was just as I expected; the most beautiful souls on earth bonded at first sight. Milana, then three years old, took the baby in her arms and held her the entire evening. Not a moment went by that she wasn't kissing her, snuggling her, and whispering in her ear, "I love you tho much, baby thiter."

Two weeks earlier, we didn't have a baby-girl name, even though Milana was set on Rainbow. I was certain I was having a baby boy, so a girl's name never crossed my mind. Thinking back now, I understand why. It was James's turn to name our daughter. Growing up, his favorite pastime was snuggling near his grandmother Sandra as she read the book *Madeline* to him and his siblings. One evening, James called me to his office and said, "How about Madelyn? I love that name."

The conversation was interrupted by a call from my mother.

"Hey, Mom, what's up?"

"Why don't you name the baby something like Madline or Madelyn?"

It was as if the angels had whispered in their ears about the perfect name for our little girl. Madelyn Alexsandra—Alex is my mother's mother, and Sandra is James's mother's mother. How lucky we were to honor two extraordinary women in our lives in one name. Alex, my grandmother in Russia, had been struggling with her health for years. I wanted so badly for her to live long enough to know how much I loved her and that I honored her, even though we parted ways when I was just seven years old. Less than one month after Madelyn was born, my grandmother suffered a stroke and, sadly, passed away on March 10, just seven days before the fifth anniversary of Juliana's death. I was grateful I'd had the chance to tell her the name we'd chosen for the baby and to tell her how much we loved her. Both grandmothers had the same reaction when we told them the middle name: "I never really liked my name, but now it sounds so beautiful. I love it."

Life with our two girls was (and still is) wonderful. I couldn't believe how much love Milana had for Madelyn. One of the most beautiful memories I have is when Madelyn was about two weeks old. Milana ran up to me, hugged my legs, and said, "Thank you tho much for my baby thiter. I love her tho much. Thank you, Mommy."

What an amazing girl she is. Instead of resenting the baby who took an enormous amount of Mommy's attention, she basked in the joy of her presence.

I let Milana hold Madelyn as often as she wanted. I made her feel like she'd gained so much by being a big sister, rather than losing all the attention. She would sing to her, play with her, and show her books and was completely by her side when she was home from daycare. I expected them to have a special bond, and to this day I am in awe of their relationship. I orchestrated their bond by allowing Milana to express her love for Madelyn in the way she felt right. She would squeeze her, hold her tight, and walk around with her, rocking her back and forth as she sang her favorite songs. Many times I wanted to drop everything and yell, "Careful," but I held back. I wanted Milana to feel that I trusted her to carefully handle Madelyn. It was that trust she felt emanate from me that gave her the confidence she needed to carefully care for her baby sister.

Madelyn didn't understand if Milana was playing too rough with her—she found it amusing—but Milana cared if I would show distrust in the way she handled her sister.

I have a very close and beautiful relationship with my brother, Max. We are so close and have an incredibly strong bond. Our love for each other is deep, and the way we understand each other's joy and problems has been a huge contributing factor to my growth. Every time we are together, he tells me (and everyone around us), "The day Kat was born was the happiest day of my life." I want my girls to have the same gift of friendship that Max and I do.

Now that they are older, they rarely argue, but when they do

I try my hardest not to step in. I know they have a mutual respect for each other, and if given the chance, they can work things out on their own. This also prevents me from creating winners and losers in an argument. Usually, the youngest child wins, giving the older one less of a chance to get her point across. And that only leads the older child to resent the younger child. They can be diplomatic, however, when there is no adult intervention. They decide who wins, not me, and often I don't even know the whole story because they usually play on their own. I love watching Milana kiss Madelyn good-bye when she goes to school. I love watching her give everything she has to make Madelyn happy. When Madelyn is being super-cute, Milana smiles as she looks at me and whispers, "Oh, my goodness, she is so cute, Mom."

Seeing Madelyn look up to her sister and love her with all her heart is the most beautiful image. Milana's eyes often light up when she is looking at Madelyn, and Madelyn squeals with joy when she is around Milana. On weekends, when everyone is together, we watch them as they play. They fill the house with laughter, speak their own language, and play their own games. I can't believe I used to feel guilty for having another baby. The biggest gift I gave my kids are siblings! I also realized I wasn't the best playmate for Milana; she didn't need my attempt to play games. She needed a sibling who understood her games.

When kids adore each other and are grateful to have each other, it contributes to the joy in the household. From the moment Madelyn came home, she slept near me, and Milana snuggled her from the back. We never spent a night apart, and I couldn't imagine a better way to spend the night. At first, I didn't want to let Madelyn sleep with us because I didn't want her to be like Milana—unable to sleep without me. But after a few nights of sweet nightly snuggles and restful sleep, thanks to my always-available breast, I couldn't hold myself back from the bliss of us all sleeping near each other. I believe something happens at night when everyone is sleeping together. An invisible bond of the souls is nourished as we lay near each other (sometimes *on* each other).

The best feeling in the world is when I snuggle Madelyn, Milana snuggles Madelyn, and James wraps his huge arms around us all. We are all together. We are all one, dreaming by each other's sides. We are there to comfort whoever has a bad dream, and it's especially soothing for me since I often wake up from nightmares, petrified of what I've dreamed. Nothing eases a horrible, heart-pounding nightmare like the beautiful warmth that is my children sleeping near me. Before I had children, nighttime for me was often an anxious time—I was no longer distracted by the day's events and finally thought about all the things that worried me. But when I hold my babies, their peaceful energy permeates my soul, allowing me to drift off to sleep to the scent of their hair, skin, and breath. My last thoughts of the day are always a heartfelt thank-you for the privilege of falling asleep in the embrace of my children. (I want to point out that there is no perfect way to sleep, whether it's with your children or without them. Always do whatever gives you the most joy and feels best to you–. That is the secret to being a happy mama, and there is nothing more important than your happiness.)

My favorite parenting is nighttime parenting. My only job is to snuggle and provide comfort. I believe that God gives us children to remind us of what's most important in life. To me, it's to blissfully be in each other's embrace. Motherhood is a gift for the purpose of fully enjoying life, not to struggle against our desires. Many mothers feel they have to follow the "rules," and they struggle with parenting. To me, motherhood is about breaking all the rules and fully enjoying every second of this privilege.

As winter was ending, James opened his own energy agency. The commissions were so high that we sometimes felt it was too good to be true. I was ready to get out of the house and make some money, but I wasn't ready to put Madelyn in daycare at only two months old. Twice a week we would get dressed and go to work. I was so comfortable with my clients that I didn't care what they thought of my walking in with a baby in my carrier. If the older clients gave me looks, I would say, "Do you know how much college costs? She is starting to work now toward saving money. All the proceeds from this commission go toward her education, and I want her to earn it."

They would laugh, and some would think I was crazy, but almost everyone signed deals with me. Madelyn was a great partner, and her super-cute face was a deal-sealer. I was in a good place in life, I was getting out, socializing, and still had my baby near me to nurse, to hold, and to spend time with. For the time being, I'd found a balance in life. I was also having a blast going away with James one night a month. My parents would take the girls and build their relationship, and James and I would build ours. I couldn't believe how crazy I'd been for preventing Milana from staying overnight at my parents' home for the first two years of her life. Maybe James and I could have had a few nights to be alone, to talk or to maybe even have sex in peace. Maybe we would be able to prevent the build-up of tension that time apart often causes. But I realize now that my desire to be supermom was much greater than my desire to be a happy mom, though my desire for happiness did begin to get stronger each day.

The more freedom I gave myself, the more everyone around me accommodated my desire—and no one thought I was less of a mother, especially not my children. I finally found a great balance in life, honoring all of my roles. When I was with the girls, I was a very attentive and happy mother. When I was with James, I was a sexy, sultry tigress who was attentive and passionate. When I was alone, I pampered myself with spa treatments and books I thought I'd not read until the kids went to college. At work, I was a super-confident, very successful sales executive.

Every month I organized family dinners to spend quality time with my brother and parents. This balance of attention toward my roles gave my life color and a variety of emotions. As everything in my life fell into place, I was able to think clearly. The stage was set for my inner voice to shine through. I was no longer distracted. I was ready to listen. I was done with excuses.

One beautiful spring day, I couldn't get out of bed. I'd just found out the night before that the energy market had crashed, and I was out of work again. I wondered why as soon as I found something I was happy with, it came crashing down. This huge blow knocked me off my feet. I sat on the steps in my backyard, thinking about what I was going to do. The more I thought about it, the worse I felt. And then I stopped thinking. I lay down and stared at the sky for an hour. I wondered why God gave me the gift of speaking, the gift of energy, and the gift of Juliana's experience and brain wiring to think differently. Why was I brought into the world? What was my purpose, and why did I wake up in the middle of the night wondering how I could make an impact globally? These thoughts had begun as whispers when I was nineteen and got louder and louder, no matter how hard I tried to shush them. Becoming a mother gave me a huge sense of purpose, but it was no longer enough. I wanted to use my gifts for something more. I dreamed of a life that did not entail door-to-door sales.

I wanted to create something. The fire within me was gaining momentum with each question I asked of the universe, Juliana, and God. Finally, I felt the urge to surrender and agree to stop forcing my destiny but to keep my eyes open for new opportunities. It was hard to see open doors when all my focus was on the closed door in front of me, so I chose to let go of my tight grip on figuring it all out and let the universe take over. I prayed, promising to watch for signs and allowing the universe to show me how I could serve my purpose.

Looking back at that very moment, it was as if a massive energy pulse was sent to the universe, and my journey into self-discovery became the focus of my life. Later that day, at dinner, James told me he had a meeting the next morning about an opportunity that might interest me. Not thinking anything of it, I went on about my evening. That night, I lay in bed, feeling as if something was about to change, but this time I had no fear. Instead, I had total and complete trust that it would be life-changing for the better.

I woke up the next day, still feeling a bit lost. Suddenly, the phone rang. It was James.

"Kat, get dressed and come to the office now. I think I just found an amazing opportunity for you."

I got there within a half hour, happy because the music in the car was unusually good and hopeful because I felt right about this new opportunity. The next series of events were direct communication from my guiding angels. The guys who ran the organization flew in from Florida that morning to share an opportunity with the owner of our temporary office space. I watched the presentation about this company called Lyoness. Of the one hundred people in the room, I felt as if the information was just for me. The company specialized in creating shopping communities by rewarding customers with cash back for their purchases from the merchants who joined the network. I would get paid a portion of every sale made within my shopping community, which would be all of New Jersey. Surely the customers would love to get cash back on their purchases, and merchants would love to reward loyal customers for choosing them. Off every sale made, a portion of the proceeds would go to benefit a not-for-profit children's fund that helped rebuild schools and hospitals in poverty-stricken areas around the world. (This was the global impact that I kept hearing in my head.) It was a win/win all around, and it sounded like a ton of fun.

I was so excited. I researched everything I could about the company. I followed my gut and welcomed this new opportunity as a sign.

The following week we decided to discuss the details with our new partner (the owner of the building) at his home in Florida. It was a beautiful, hot day, and we all decided to go to the pool. Milana was having a blast jumping in and out of the pool, and then I saw her give me the sign that she had to go the bathroom. After we returned, we saw a woman at the pool, and I noticed something about her that made my mouth drop. She had the Lyoness company logo tattooed on her wrist. I felt this was a sign.

I stopped her and said, "I'm sorry to bother you, but what is that tattoo on your wrist, and what does it mean?"

She explained that it was an Irish symbol that connected her sister in heaven, the living world, and her together. They were one, always communicating, and she lived her life following the guidance of her sister. I was speechless and could only think that if Juliana could come down in human form, she would shake me, telling me, "Yes, Lyoness is what you should be doing." I was so grateful for this insight, and the more I looked for signs, the more they showed up in very clear form. I spent the summer studying loyalty programs and creating my plan of attack.

I felt so much freedom to do things the way I felt was right and to try things without fear of failure. I kept pushing myself, squeezing every bit of creativity out of me. I was grateful that I could build something without needing to make immediate profit. People often are unable to take advantage of an opportunity because they are committed to their jobs and must rely on the income they receive to make ends meet. If I was given an opportunity to create something and to build something of enormous value without worrying about making immediate money, then surely I was going to give it my all.

It was such an exhilarating time in my life. I was completely consumed with figuring out how to create a harmonious shopping community in which everyone would win. People were coming in to my life who were just as excited about this opportunity as I was, and we spent many nights together, dreaming about the future.

In August, I got a phone call from Matt, the guy who introduced us to Lyoness. He was having enormous success in Fort Lauderdale and thought it would be great for me to come down for a few weeks to make money and to get a feel for how it worked when numerous merchants were involved. I packed my car, found a daycare for the girls in Fort Lauderdale, and headed down without a plan for when I would return. We were lucky to be close friends with Matt and his wife, Sandra. Staying in their home was always fun for the girls and me. It was an exciting time for me—the signs were everywhere, assuring me that I was on the right path. Even though I had no success thus far, I felt good about what I was doing and didn't allow failure to distract me.

Then, one incredibly hot morning, Sandra and I were having breakfast at an upscale coffee shop. I was planning my day, but I felt too hot to walk and was almost discouraged. As I looked around, I saw something that changed me forever. I saw people enjoying their breakfasts, having light conversations, and planning their days with joy-filled activities. Their faces were calm and smiling, and I got the sense that they knew something I didn't. I wondered why I couldn't live a life like this. *Why can't I enjoy life right now?* I thought. *Why do I always feel that I have to work hard so that one day, I too can enjoy a long breakfast or even a day filled with joyful activities, rather than guilt for not working? Why is my desire to be "someone" so much stronger than my desire to live and enjoy the moment?*

I wondered if it was my obsession with being financially safe so that I wouldn't live like my stressed, overworked, financially unstable parents. Though James was a great provider, I wanted to rely on myself for financial stability. What did these people do that they could enjoy life on this level—and how could I live this way? Was there a secret? Had I been doing it all wrong, chasing the wrong dream?

I felt as if those people were perfectly positioned there so that I could have this epiphany. Everything at that moment felt surreal, as if I was in a dream and was forced to pay attention. They didn't even look like real people but more like avatars, carrying out a mission. My face froze, and it was as if a seed had been planted within me, waiting to be watered, wanting to grow. I spent the day thinking about what had happened at the coffee shop. I desperately knocked on doors, wanting to convince business owners to join the shopping community, but unfortunately, everyone said no. Never in my ten years in sales had I experienced such devastation. Business owners seemed to like me and love what I was selling, but they refused to sign deals with me. Sandra and I couldn't take it anymore, and we decided to have a drink at the next place we could find.

After a few blocks of walking in the hundred-degree heat, we finally saw a nice restaurant and walked inside to cool off in the air conditioning. We ordered lunch and mojitos. As we talked, sipping on the delicious mojitos, we tried to laugh off our lack of success. Then a group of five gentlemen walked in. They saw our pamphlets and asked us what we were selling. Within a few minutes, we were sitting at their table, explaining Lyoness. We got along really well, and they seemed to have a close relationship with most of the merchants we were going after. It seemed to be a God-sent meeting. The next day we met for lunch at a restaurant where we wanted to do business and were introduced to the owner. It was a sunny day, and the breeze blowing off the bay was magnificent.

During a discussion about life, one of the gentlemen asked me, "How do you do what you do? You are so good at it."

I didn't know what he meant, but I replied, "I just do; I don't know."

He smiled. "So you know the book *The Secret*. I live by it too. Isn't it amazing?"

I looked at his calm, happy, satisfied-with-life face. Then I took in the view of the bay, looked around me, and realized we were in the middle of a workday, enjoying this gorgeous atmosphere, but all I could feel was guilt for talking rather than working. I felt embarrassed because I didn't know what he was talking about. I didn't know the "secret"; all I knew was I had to get back to pounding the pavement—back to getting nowhere but still trying my hardest. Sandra and I excused ourselves and left, and something within me wanted to run to the nearest Barnes & Noble to find this book called *The Secret*.

Within twenty-four hours, my entire belief system was shaken up. I experienced surreal circumstances that seemed to be desperately trying to teach me something. My desire to understand the signs was overridden by my desire to do what I knew—hard work, which is the only way to get results. When I picked up the girls from daycare, they looked happy, but I saw the muddy backyard where they were spending their days. I was done with Florida. I needed to get back home. I felt like I got what I'd come there for. My eyes were now wide open to a life that was far different from my working-class parents' lifestyle. It was far different from anything I had ever seen. It was as if I was meant to experience a different dimension that would entice me to keep exploring this "secret." I felt as if I was called to go on the journey to discover the secret to life's bliss for which I had been yearning all my life.

While still in Florida, I woke up one morning feeling unusually sick and nauseated. I felt like I'd been tumbling in a car wreck all night; everything part of my body hurt. I looked down and noticed my belly was swollen. Thinking I was just gaining weight from eating all the "yumminess" that Florida had to offer, I dismissed it. As the day progressed, I felt more and more nauseated. Having been in this situation more than once, I decided to take a pregnancy test. I starred at it, thinking, *How strong-willed does this soul have to be if I only had one period since giving birth to Madelyn* (thanks to nursing), *which was over eighteen months ago?*

The test not only indicated I was pregnant but that I was two to three weeks. I sat on the toilet, thinking what had happened 2.5 weeks earlier. I was sure we were being safe. Then I remembered; it was one of the most extraordinary days. Since my brother and I first saw Cinderella, an eighties rock band, in concert on TV in 1989, we had been obsessed with their music. The way the singer and guitarist hits notes made me feel it in the depth of my soul. Throughout my life, during good times and bad, I would listen to their songs. I always felt like he was speaking to me, using the exact words I needed to hear, strumming his guitar and hitting notes I needed to feel. For twenty-five years I knew exactly what I would say to him if I ever saw him.

On July 29, Max's birthday, we got tickets to see the band

perform their classic hits at an intimate bar in New York City. I was watching Tom, the lead singer, from a few feet away as he sang the songs that brought out such emotion in me. It was as if the universe was showing me the power of dreams and the unusual way they manifest. I'd dreamed of this day since I was five years old—being face-to-face with my musical idol. I would often joke with James that if I ever had a chance to "rock out" with Tom, it didn't count as cheating. (Not sure if he agreed, but a girl can dream.)

After the show, I was able to go backstage and finally give Tom a hug. I told him how much his music had shaped my life and that I'd been introduced to them as Cinderella before learning of the story of the princess. I thanked him for sharing his voice and not keeping his gift from the world. It was such an incredible moment for me. Dreams I once thought were impossible were now showing me their possibilities. That night, with every cell in my body still in awe of the amazing night we'd had, a beautiful soul desired to come into existence.

The girls and I took the train on our return from Florida. I booked a private coupe. When I was little, I used to love sleeping on bunk beds as I listened to the train move. I shared all my childhood stories with the girls as we snuggled, falling asleep together to the sound of the train moving. *Ta-ta ta-tan ta-ta ta-tan.* The train lulled us all into a deep sleep—sleep my pregnant body thoroughly enjoyed.

When I got back, I went straight to work; I squeezed every bit of creativity out of myself once more. Finally, after weeks of not getting anywhere, I felt the urge to go to a bookstore to find any inspiration I could so I would keep working and keep pushing. I looked for books that told stories of people accomplishing the impossible or overcoming immense obstacles. I was desperate to find anything that would give me reasons to keep my flame burning with hope. As if by some miracle, I was waiting for my coffee at the Starbucks counter when I noticed that someone had left a book near the cash register. I picked it up and felt weak in the knees when I read the title: *The Secret*.

Oh, my God. I had forgotten about this book that the gentlemen in Florida had mentioned. I didn't even have to browse the bookshelves; the universe presented the golden ticket—a free fast pass to allow me to leap forward. I began reading it and was absolutely consumed by it, as if it was written for me at my exact place in life. Every word resonated with me. Though the concepts were new to me, it awoke a knowing within me. Somehow, I completely understood and knew what the author was trying to say, even though it was a language that was very foreign to me. It was as if my logical mind was saying, *It's all bullshit*, but my soul was remembering it was the exact truth for which I had been desperately looking. I read half the book before it was time to pick up the girls from daycare. I bought the CD version so I could listen on my way home. I didn't want to miss this God-sent opportunity to find the answer I'd looked for my entire life.

The premise of the book is that our thoughts and feelings control the world around us. More important, our belief systems control what we attract. When we are desperately trying to make something work, we send out a signal to the universe, which in turn gives us more desperation. When we change our thinking and believe that our dreams are meant to become our reality, things happen at much faster speeds. The book also gave me the understanding that we attract what we *are*, not what we want. For example, if we are happy and joyful with life, we attract events, people, and circumstances that enhance our joy and happiness. In other words, we are walking, breathing magnets, and the world around us has manifested through the law of attraction. Our thoughts and belief systems have attracted everything in our lives. This is why complainers always have plenty of circumstances to complain about. Those who live from a place of gratitude and love always have plenty to rejoice and feel grateful for.

It all seemed so simple but still so new to me. The biggest game changer for me was to live from a place of being grateful that all I want is already in my life. When you pray and ask for things from a place of wanting, you are emitting a signal to the universe that you are lacking something. The universe responds with a yes for everything you are feeling but not asking for. And so you find yourself lacking the things you want. Changing the way you ask—or rather, the way you pray—is the single biggest difference between staying in a state of wanting and celebrating the manifestation of that which you want. The correct way to ask and pray is, *I am so grateful that the universe always provides me with abundance in love, joy, and money. Thank you for always giving me more than I ask for. Thank you for always making all my dreams my reality. Thank you for always taking care of those I love so much.*

Prayers like that emit a signal to the universe that you are already grateful for that which you desire, and so your desire begins to move into your reality. I learned that the universe uses the language of feeling rather than speaking. This is why when I asked for things from a place of hope—*I hope this client signs the deal with me. I hope we have enough to pay the bills*—the universe always responded with more reasons to stay hopeful but not the actual manifestation of what I asked for.

Many prayers also come from a place of worry and frustration and often are answered with more worrying and frustrating circumstances. This is why no matter how much you worry and no matter how much sleep you lose through worrying, the outcome is often more reasons to keep worrying. The universe—or God; however you want to refer to it—always answers you with a yes.

Making money is hard work—the universe responds with "yes, it is," and makes sure you work your butt off to make money.

Parenting is hard; my kids never seem to listen to me. Parents who feel that way often have difficult children who don't listen to them.

I'll never lose this weight and have the body I dream of. My metabolism is slow and so is weight loss. These are the people who often stay overweight and battle weight loss their entire lives.

This whole Secret thing is bullshit. Life is not and can't be that easy. For the person who thinks this way, life will never stop showing them reasons that support their thinking. Change your thinking and expectations to thoughts that serve you, rather than harm you. It takes the same amount of effort to think, *I have this. Life is always good to me,* as it does to think, *I am always getting screwed by life. If it weren't for bad luck, I wouldn't have any luck at all.*

So why waste your thoughts on producing negative emotions rather than those that are positive? The happiest, wealthiest, and luckiest people on the planet did not get there by worrying or by feeling like victims. They got there by changing their belief systems with regard to what they believe they deserve to receive. Your life is a reflection of what you think about, so look around—what can you change? Changing your thoughts will change your entire world!

Another new concept for me was "Ask, Believe, and Receive." Ask for what you want, believe in every cell of your body that it's manifesting in your life, and then receive it. *Wait … what?* I thought. *How about planning? How about figuring things out? How about staying up all night thinking of a clear plan on how to bring that which I want into my life?* Apparently, if you want something, and you believe you are truly worthy of receiving it, the universe rearranges itself to bring it into your life. Don't worry about the details of how it will manifest; just believe and act on intuition as you follow the signs that will bring it forth in your life. This is why some of the most amazing events and circumstances that ever happen to us come unplanned and seemingly out of nowhere. This was by far the hardest concept for me, an avid planner and control freak, to accept. It would be another year before I really understood the power of this notion.

I realized that everything I knew about life was completely wrong. That tugging feeling I had that I was created to live a life filled with joy, blissful emotions, and millions of reason to smile was my soul speaking to me. The force that brought me into the world intended for me to live at the highest level of euphoria, not at the lowest level of suffering. Life is not meant to be lived in fear or overwhelmed with worry, pain, or guilt. I didn't have to work myself to exhaustion, desperately trying to make something work and begging God to turn the hearts of clients so that I could have success. I was forcing everything around me: that's why nothing was happening—except more opportunities and reasons to keep forcing things to work.

I worked forty hours a week for months without making any progress or a single dollar. The worse my outcome was, the worse I felt about it. I was holding my desire to succeed by the throat, suffocating it and shutting off the power of the universe to work its magic on my behalf. The book *The Secret* speaks of tipping the scale of luck. When your car breaks down, you feel annoyed and worried about the additional unexpected expense. That emotion you emit to the universe is irritability and worry about how to find the money to repair the car. Usually, on the day you lose a major client the feeling gets worse and invites more negative events that continue the horrible unexpected circumstances. If it works for bad situations, surely the same law applies to good ones. This explains why when I was grateful and happy for positive events, more good things happened, and at one point I felt like luck was befriending me. I tipped the scale. I felt more joy than worry. Then, when I tipped the scale again by feeling like nothing was working out, things began to go downhill. I understood that allowing negative circumstances to bother me deeply is what triggered the scales to bring me back into an array of negative experiences. I listened to the audio book in my car obsessively, over and over again for weeks. At first it was hard to believe, but the more I listened, the more I began to see from daily experiences that this was the exact way the world worked.

I played tricks with this new information, wanting to assure myself that this was the only way the universe worked and accepting that there was absolutely no other way. My biggest moment happened when I heard the following words: "Everything you have been through, all the information you have received, all the events that transpired in your life have prepared you for this moment of receiving this very information." As I sat in my car, listening to these words, I was watching a magnificent sunset. I felt as if I was perfectly positioned in front of this extraordinary display of colors and was watching it with brand-new eyes. Unable to hold back tears, I sobbed uncontrollably.

My whole life flashed before my eyes. I saw all the events that led me to understand what life had been attempting to show me—from being a little girl in yeshiva, learning about God, to registering for a particular class in college, only to find it was full, forcing me to take a class called "Levels of Consciousness," where I was introduced to the concept of the universe, one of the biggest eye-opening classes of my life. I saw myself paralyzed with fear that Juliana would die when she was a few weeks old. I saw the times when, in a single year, all my fears became my reality, as well as all the times when my dreams became my reality, though much better than I could have imagined. My entire life supported everything the book described, and I knew it was time for a major change in my thinking, even my understanding of money.

I don't have a lot of money. Making money is a constant struggle and will always be a burden. I don't come from money, and so my chances of making a lot of it are low. I had instilled in me a belief that paying bills was a stressful time, mortgages suffocated all those who chose to take them on, and money was the root of all evil. No wonder money hated me (though, thankfully, it loved James). Money probably said something like, "Well, we cause her so much pain and anxiety we should just leave her alone. Come on; let's all leave her so that she won't have any more stress."

As I dived deeper, I realized that it was the conditioning, the paradigm, and my belief system that controlled my life. I could think positive thoughts, but if I didn't believe them to be true, then no amount of positive thinking would help. I had to change my conditioning, and I could do that by changing the way I believed things to be. The new "laws" of life that I was learning were blowing my mind, and no matter how unrealistic they seemed, I knew deep within me that they were true. I finally understood the secret of those peaceful, relaxed people I'd seen in Florida. They drowned their thoughts in joy and were able to live an amazing life, where struggle was as foreign to them as a sense of ease was to me.

My entire life unraveled before me, showing me the secret I always had known but couldn't understand. My mornings used to begin with waking up and thinking of all the things I had to get done. The anxiety caused by that to-do list was what propelled me out of bed. Now, I was waking up with a smile, grateful to have the gift of life and blissfully excited to spend my day with a sense of purpose, even if it was just to show my love to the rain that watered my flowers (a huge time-saver for me). Instead of writing the things I had to get done, I wrote all the things in my life for which I was grateful and treasured deeply. Within a few mornings of doing this, everything began to fall into place. Thanksgiving was a week away, and I felt that was a sure sign I was on the right path to spiritual growth. But this was just the beginning.

Chapter 9

I was sent to get a detailed ultrasound to see how the baby was developing and to confirm the due date. Just as I was getting dressed, the doctor came in to go over what he saw.

"Can I have this ultrasound picture for our wall?" he asked. "The *schmeckel* on your boy is impressive."

What? I didn't want to find out the sex. We usually left it as a surprise. Then it hit me like a ton of bricks: my vision of holding a baby boy, which I'd had from the moment I was pregnant with my first baby, was now going to be a reality. I loved my girls, but after three I kind of wanted a change of scenery, if you know what I mean. Knowing that this was my last baby, I wanted to tell James and the girls in a special way. I bought a blue blanket that was held by a white plush bear and put it in a box wrapped in beautiful paper. Once everyone got home, I said, "I have a gift for you all." I handed the girls the box, and they tore through the wrapping paper.

Milana finally opened the box and said, "Yay! We are having a baby bear." I looked at James's reaction; he was happy and excited because he swore we were having another girl, although to him, any baby, regardless of gender, was reason to celebrate.

When Milana realized we were having a baby boy, she said, "We finally have Olaf for Halloween next year. I am Elsa, Madelyn is Anna, and all we needed was a boy. This is perfect."

I couldn't stop laughing at how she viewed having a baby brother.

We all did the tightest, longest group hug; we squeezed each other until we couldn't breathe. Our home was filled with so much joy and excitement, feeling grateful was easier than ever.

Thanksgiving was a lovely day at our home. Our families came together, and everyone recited long lists of all they were grateful for. Milana's list brought tears to my eyes. "I am thankful for the trees that make our street pretty," she said. "I am thankful for my sister, who is so cute I want to squeeze her. I am thankful for my mommy not being sick. I am thankful for my daddy being big and reaching all the high places to get me things. I am grateful for my whole family being fun." At age five she was already living the fundamental value of *The Secret*—an attitude of gratitude!

I always heard that people, toward the end of their lives, realize that the most important gift with which we humans have been bestowed is love. Love is the source, creation, and nourishment of all that is alive. Humans couldn't exist without love. Love is what compels the act of lovemaking (even if not love for the person involved then surely for the act itself). Love is the force that compels the sperm and the egg to merge and divide perfectly. Love is in everything that brings joy. The only true power on earth is the power of love.

I never really understood love. I always thought it was an emotion felt for a child, a mother, and a spouse or lover. It was a warm, fuzzy feeling that brought joy to me for a moment. Love, for me, often was associated with pain, anxiety, and worry. My love for my brother, who was struggling with his own demons, caused a lot of emotional pain for me. My love for the finer things and the lack of it in my life also often was a source of anxiety. My love for my children was the reason why I worried so much.

Now, I felt compelled to study everything I could about this energy, this most powerful human emotion. What I found was absolutely mind-blowing. Love is the most natural, easiest emotion to feel on a daily basis, and it is this emotion that will bring everything that is magnificent in the world into your life. When you spend your days thinking about only what you love, the universe will flood your life with more things for you to love and think about. When you spend your days finding all that you love in the environment around you, it will give you more things to love about your world. When you focus on all the things you love about a human being, you will keep seeing more reasons to love that person. When all you talk about is what you love, you will have more of what you love to talk about. It is the single biggest secret of the law of attraction that helps manifest a life you will love. When you choose to see your life through the veil of love, you will find yourself in a magnificent world. When you see something you love but can't have, the key is to still feel love, as the law of attraction will begin to work to bring it to you. Focus in every situation only on what you love, and the things you dislike will begin to quickly dissipate. If you want to lose weight, send love to your body and thank it for being so perfect. When you see a couple in love and happy, send them love, and you will magnetize the same relationship for yourself.

As I began to implement the law of love into my life, I spent most of my time in awe of all that surrounded me. I realized that my language was my biggest enemy, and so I focused on using words that activated the energy of love within me and around me. When I focused on all that I loved in my conversations, suddenly I had very little to complain about.

I began to correct Milana when she would tell me about her day and complaining was the main topic of conversation. The typical conversation would begin with, "I don't like this" or "I really hate that," but I would stop her and say, "Only speak of what you love. What did you love about your day?" Within weeks, her language and mood completely changed. She smiled more and seemed to find endless reasons to talk about all she loved. We have a rule in the house that she can't use the word hate. Sometimes she slips and says "the H word," but she often corrects herself when she sees how disappointed I am and how badly she feels.

I stopped feeling anxiety and bitterness almost instantly when all my conversations with James shifted to discussions of all that we love. Previously, our discussions would start with comments such as, "I can't believe this guy said ..."; "That guy is a moron"; "This house is always a mess"; or "The kids don't listen." When James and I would start venting, I realized it didn't make us feel better; it actually made us feel much worse. We would talk about a frustrating circumstance at work, and it would catapult into a two-hour bitching session about everything from the government to the ant problem we couldn't seem to get under control.

As I began to implement love into all that I thought about and spoke of, our conversations began to change. If James would begin with "I can't believe this asshole," I would interrupt him by saying, "Did you see the way Milana helped Madelyn play?" Then his emotions would shift to a more positive light, and our conversation would become exclamations of all that was wonderful in our lives. We actually accomplished more when we used our alone time to express our love and gratitude for all our blessings. The more we spoke about our blessings, the more our lives flooded with blessings to speak about. The less we spoke about our lack of money and more about our financial opportunities, the more those lucrative opportunities came into our lives. Within a few months, we had very little to vent about, even if we tried. It felt wrong and weird to even bring up negative situations.

I even mastered the art of guiding other people's conversations away from discussing negative circumstances and toward positive ones. When someone would complain about the economy, I would reply, "There are more billionaires today than ever before, I love the financial opportunities we get these days." Or if someone said, "It's freezing. I hate the cold," I would reply, "I love this weather. The air is so cold and so fresh I can smell snow. It reminds me of when I was a little girl and didn't have much of an opinion on weather." People seemed to shift according to my energy. When I was feeling love for all that is around me, I attracted people who felt the same way I did. This, of course, resulted in my losing many childhood friends who thought I was "living in the clouds" and losing my mind. But looking back, it was a beautiful cleansing process, necessary for me to live the life I wanted. It was rare to be riding the frequency of love and joy and come across someone who was at the lowest end of the frequency level. The law of attraction would have a very hard time attracting the two spectrums.

I began to realize that the more I lived from a place of love, the more the universe thanked me for seeing its magnificence, and the more it rewarded me with experiences that kept me in a state of awe, in a state of gratitude, and in a state of love.

For example, in New York City I am always amazed by the hundred-floor apartment buildings. Those living on the lower floors rarely get to see the magnificence of New York City sunsets, as do those who live on the top floors. The sunset is magnificent, regardless of whether someone on the lower levels sees it or not, but only those on the top get to see it in all its glory. Change your thinking to see the world through the eyes of love, and you too can see life from the top.

Since I was a little girl, I always had a feeling that sunsets were a gift from God to remind us of beauty and to be completely in awe of the magnificence of nature. No matter where I was, I always went toward a window or outside to watch the sky change colors at sunset. I always wished to live in a home that had at least one window that faced west so that I could enjoy watching the sun setting every evening. The home we live in offers views of awe-inspiring sunsets. Being up on a hill, we have the privilege of seeing the sun set until it descends below the horizon. I had watched the sun go down many times from our windows, but I never really connected with it. *The Secret* teaches that you should ask for a sign from the universe that will surely get your attention, reminding you to reset your emotions and have a moment of grateful prayer for all that happened during the day. It's as if the sun wanted to get my attention, because every evening I somehow was placed perfectly—in front of a window or on a road if I was driving—to marvel at the changing colors. Sometimes when I was away on a trip, James would send me pictures of the sun setting through our windows or from the backyard. I never asked him to do that; he just felt inspired to do so.

Often during a sunset, I would grab Milana and tell her to say "Thank you for my beautiful day" as the sun changed the color of the sky. Almost always, when she did her prayers, the sky would turn a pinkish color. She would smile with excitement as if it was a sign for her from the sky, since pink is her favorite color. I only had to do this a few times before she would call to me when she caught a glimpse of the sun setting and ask me to stand with her. We both would smile and pray.

Christmas at our home was a festival of lights. One day, I decided to decorate everything in bright white lights. I had the urge to make the outside of our home as beautiful and as bright as possible, hoping that someone who was struggling during this season might find joy in the twinkling display. I began to live for others with the intention of making them feel the joy I did. I did not expect anything in return, and that was my biggest shift. I used to give from an anxious heart, fearing I wouldn't receive a similarly beautiful gift or that someone wouldn't return a favor. I would decorate with hope of showing others how much we were capable of (often monetarily). This time, however, I was decorating to bring beauty to those who saw my creations. I realized that I had wanted to give throughout my entire life, but when I did, I felt as if I had less left for me. I misunderstood the concept of sacrificing for others rather than sharing all that I was overflowing with.

When Milana was little, and James was gone for fifteen hours a day, I sacrificed for him and her. I emitted a signal that came not from an abundance of love or joy but from lack thereof. That's why things kept taking a negative turn. I felt resentful for giving up my happiness and my freedom, rather than grateful for the privilege of having so much within me to give.

People may feel that if they sacrifice for others, they will be repaid. But giving from a heart that is overflowing with love means there is little need for anything in return. The greatest return is the gratification of seeing your heart influence another human being. I finally mastered the art of giving away love without feeling less of it and giving beautiful gifts without feeling like I was depleting our budget. My main focus and intention was to bring joy to the people of the world, even if for a split second. Somehow, the more I gave from the heart, the more I was flooded with gifts from the universe.

I felt like a magician—everything I needed and wanted manifested almost instantly.

Every day I had new realizations. I felt as if my "knowing" was my remembering information from past lives. I wanted so badly to share with the world my newfound knowledge. Everyone on earth deserves to know that life is about bliss, not struggle. Everything is in your mind; whatever you believe to be true will manifest in your life. Whether you believe what I am saying is true or not, you're right either way. It's shockingly that simple. My thoughts were once my biggest enemy. They paralyzed me, preventing my enjoying life and stifling my empowerment to keep smiling at the magic all around me.

Nothing in my life changed except my perception of it. Every day, my thoughts morphed from worry to gratitude. By New Year's Eve, the most important day of the year for me, I was at the tipping point of feeling more love than judgment, more light than darkness. It was as if all my dreams already had come true, rather than my hoping for things to work out. This is very important—positive thoughts do not manifest our desires. I was confused for years because I assumed that a thought of hope was positive, so it should have a huge impact on my life. I had hopeful thoughts, thinking they were positive. All I got in return, however, were more reasons to have hopeful thoughts, rather than reasons to celebrate the manifestation of whatever I hoped for.

To celebrate the new year, I wanted to create a feast of delicious foods for my family. On the way to the store, I reviewed my year, financially and career-wise. I realized I'd made no headway. But spiritually and emotionally, I was elevating on a daily basis. I realized that I couldn't have made money or had success in having clients sign up as part of the shopping community I was so desperately trying to build. My focus was on hope, and the more feelings of hope I sent out, the more reasons I had to be hopeful. Things would almost work out … but not actually work out. It was as if success was on a fishing hook, right before me, giving me plenty of reasons to keep working but not really meant to work out.

I listened to an audio book called *Hero*. It's about the call to go on the "Hero's Journey" and about following your bliss, your calling. The author spoke of creating dreams, designing every aspect of them, and going after them wholeheartedly. It suddenly dawned on me that Lyoness was not the dream I created. The financial outcome was my dream but not the actual road I wanted to take. I didn't own it; the CEO of the company owned the dream. It was his vision and his bliss that he was following. That's why he was making an enormous amount of money and living the best life he'd chosen for himself.

That was the price I had to pay for being too scared to discover my bliss; I lived with the curse of not getting over the fear of being the sole architect of my dream. I thought, *Who do I think I am to dream big? I don't know anyone who can help propel me in the world.* To be more honest, I thought, *I don't have the balls to dream big because I am not worthy.* With my fearful thinking, I attached myself to other people's dreams because it was safe. If I messed it up, it wasn't on me; it was on the person whose dream I was helping to make a reality. Failure of someone else wouldn't hurt nearly as much as failure I am responsible for.

On my first day of my first real job, the insurance company where I met James, the CEO introduced me to a concept that has stayed with me over the years: You either work for someone to make that person's dream a reality, or you have people working for you to help you manifest your vision. There is little space in between, especially for a black-and-white thinking person like I am. I was taught that dreams come true for a very small percentage of people. The odds were against me, I thought, so I should just play it safe with a corporate job.

So what was my dream or my calling? I decided that my goal for 2015 would be to figure out my true bliss, without judging it if it was crazy or if it was doable. It was that New Year's Eve that I made a conscious decision to truly listen to my heart's yearning desires. I was running out of excuses I'd created for myself as to why I couldn't pursue my own dream. Yes, I was pregnant, but somehow it didn't suffice as a reason to shush my inner voice. Yes, I had two little kids to care for, but again, I no longer accepted that as valid—I couldn't keep hiding behind the "I am a mother with little kids. I can't possibly pursue my dreams now" excuse. I was more fearful of not pursuing my dream than pursuing and failing.

This was right around the time that James's grandmother passed away. She was a woman who died with so many dreams but also with excuses for not making them happen. When you run out of legitimate reasons to accept your excuses for putting your inner desires on the back burner, only then can you begin the journey toward the life for which you are the sole architect. I was so sick of myself, of the excuses, and of lowering my flame of desire because of my fear of failure. It was as if I'd seen the door before me all those years but had been too afraid to open it and discover what was behind it.

Lyoness was falling apart slowly. I knew it, but I refused to believe it; I hoped my gut instinct was wrong, even though it's never wrong. *It's never, ever, ever wrong!* And the more I thought about my dream of creating a perfectly functioning shopping community— where business owners could build their businesses and customers benefit from choosing those merchants—the more I saw that one person could not do it all. I accepted that one person—me—no longer wanted to do it all. I believed that it would work, but no one else did. Trying hard to suppress this realization, I celebrated New Year's Eve with my family, toasting to living our dreams in 2015. Deep inside I felt like I needed to get away, to meditate, and to swim in warm waters. I wanted to leave freezing New Jersey to clear my mind.

The law of attraction works solely off our energy and frequency, and the urge to raise my frequency flashed through my mind. James booked a two-week trip to Mexico and Disney World on January 1, while the girls and I were sleeping and dreaming of a vacation in paradise. We were flying out on January 12—that's how fast things worked for me. I was working the art of manifestation like a magician.

In Mexico, I basked in the bliss of the crystal-clear turquoise waters. I thanked every drop of the sea for caressing my body and cleansing my soul. The sea came alive right before my eyes. I felt such a connection to nature. One afternoon I was swimming and almost cried, as I was overwhelmed with gratitude for the joy I was feeling. The water caressed my achy twenty-six-weeks-pregnant belly, and I felt Juliana's love in the water with each gentle wave. I made plans to come back with James very soon, I wanted to be alone with him to talk and to snuggle. I loved being there with the girls, but something inside me desired intimacy with the man I loved so much.

As I was walking out of the water, James signaled to me to come back to the room. He'd just received word that he was going to be the best man for his friend's wedding … in Greece the following July. I couldn't help but smile. *Wow, that was fast! Thank you, universe, for hearing me.* The timing was perfect too because it would be three months after I gave birth to our boy, just enough time for me to bond with him and pump enough milk to last while I was gone.

I realized that I formerly spent my days yo-yoing between frequencies; that was why I had good and bad moments. I would feel joy, but then if something didn't go my way, I felt frustration. As my frequency went up and down, so did the events around me.

If you notice people are not smiling at you or things are not working out in an unusual series of events, that means it's time to do an emotional check. Are you emitting love and joy or frustration and worry? As soon as you catch yourself feeling frustrated, bring yourself back by taking twenty deep breaths. One of my coaches recommended I do this, and it's been very effective for releasing tension. I always count my blessings on my fingers; my hands are a constant reminder to do so. Once I count five blessings God has bestowed upon me, I am back to the highest frequency, where everything and everyone works to serve me. It was hard playing with frequencies all day, but the more I did it, the easier it got. When things wouldn't work out, I wouldn't allow myself to worry or feel frustration. I would use the circumstance as a friendly reminder to bring myself back up. It was an entirely new world for me. I paid attention to every detail of my surroundings, finding so much to rejoice about. In return, the universe kept giving me more reasons to feel amazing.

As soon as we got back home, Lyoness took a major turn, announcing huge changes. I had to fly to Miami headquarters to meet the CEO; it was around the time of my thirty-second birthday in February. (I guess I kept emitting a signal of wanting a little warmth.) Just before I left, James and I got into a heated discussion about what I would do if I found out things about the company that I didn't like. For example, what would I do if I found out that all my time and effort was for nothing because the company had no intention of rewarding me for my work? What if it was just a big hoax?

Then James said something that left me unable to sleep the entire night: "Maybe you should leave freelance sales and go into corporate America. You could get a job anywhere. You are so good at sales. Get a salary. Have an office. Get some structure in your life."

Oh, my God, I thought. *What a horrible life that would be.* I didn't want structure, and I didn't want a limit on how much money

I could make by having a salary. I honestly didn't want to work for money. I wanted to create something that would benefit the world and, of course, that would supply a source of income for me.

Besides, it was hard to expend effort in working for money when I already had enough of it. The sacrifice just wouldn't make sense. I didn't want to go back to work with James. His company was *his* baby, and I wanted to create something on my own. I wanted to build a business without needing instant results, allowing it to grow without stressing me. I wanted to keep nourishing my soul and keep living out my desires. I didn't want to sit in traffic, work on mundane projects which required little of my God-given gifts, sit in traffic some more, get home and rush to make dinner, and then hope that the kids went to bed early enough so that I could stare at the TV to forget the stress of my day. And the two-week limit for vacation also was a devastating thought.

I wanted to spend my days reading and learning more about the secrets to life. I wanted the freedom to live on my terms. I wanted to travel. I wanted to talk with others about how amazing life was because they shared my awe. I wanted to create something without restrictions and without "company policy" slowing me down. I wanted to live my life doing only what I was passionate about and whatever would allow my God-given gifts to shine. Above all, I wanted to serve humanity, to live my purpose, to give my gifts, and to focus on helping those who were struggling in areas where I once struggled. I wanted to wake up and know that I was making a difference in the world—or in at least one person's world. I already was beginning to understand that making money was not about struggle. Money could come from many sources; it was all about being creative.

I stayed up that night, staring at the ceiling, dreaming of the life I wanted to live—but there was still no need to think of plan B; plan A was still in effect.

I arrived in Miami and finally got to meet the man behind the dream I was tirelessly working to make a reality. We were sitting in a gorgeous office, and all the top people in the company were discussing Lyoness. All of a sudden, as if I got struck by lightning, I saw people I would never do business with. They were nowhere near the visionaries I thought they were. I realized that I was the visionary. They had an idea, but I had run with it. *Holy shit*, I thought. *If I can work so hard with so much energy and passion to make someone else's dream a reality, what can I do for my own dream?*

A year earlier I'd had a vision of walking up on stage to receive my award for reaching the highest level of commissions at the March Lyoness event in Las Vegas. I saw my name flashing on the huge screen as fireworks burst all around me. This was my biggest dream—to achieve enough so that I could get on stage to inspire others to believe and keep dreaming. I was evidence that dreams do come true. I even wrote the beginning of my speech: "First and foremost, thank you to all those who believed in my vision. I will spend my life in deepest gratitude for your trust."

I would get so overwhelmed with emotion in my vision that I sometimes would tear up as I saw James and the girls' teary eyes look at me with pride. All the sacrifice—the days I missed dinner, and the girls going to a new state and a new daycare they didn't like—would all be worth that one moment when Mommy could influence and be an inspiration to others. That dream of being on stage to inspire and ignite fires within people was why I was working tirelessly, not the concept of the company.

I spent my birthday as if it was my first—I was a brand new person. I felt as if I had been reborn, and everything I had ever learned, done, and felt was given to me solely for the realization that I was meant for something bigger than me. The universe perfectly guided me to this knowledge. That's why nothing ever worked out for me; it was all meant to fail so that I would come to that conference room to realize my potential. I understood why I'd worked fifty hours a week for a year without any success. If I had merchants in the shopping community that were thriving, it would be horrible to leave them. I would have to leave the city where I lived from the sheer embarrassment and probably harassment from all the people who wanted their money back. I felt so grateful that I'd had no success. I had the freedom to move on to my next project: project Katerina.

Sandra and I celebrated my birthday at my favorite restaurant in Fort Lauderdale. The epiphany was still raw, and I had a very hard time expressing the shift I was feeling. I smiled, laughed, and jokingly expressed my frustration with the biggest project I'd ever taken on. But deep inside, I already had something else brewing. I just didn't know what it was.

I came back home to tell James that Lyoness was no longer the company that would be our ticket out. But I also told him that our dreams didn't have to be downgraded. I just needed time to figure out my next move. The company James built was giving us our dream lifestyle, but looking back, the dream was more about living to our fullest potential and to keep striving and working on becoming the best version of ourselves, without limits or borders.

Chapter 10

I was thirty-four weeks pregnant in March, right around the time of the Lyoness event in Vegas that I had fantasized about. My days were spent in Barnes & Noble, reading books by others who felt the urge that they were destined for something big. One day, on my way to the bookstore, I was listening to Dr. Wayne Dyer talk about interpreting signs all around us. I was already a big believer in this phenomenon, and I felt there was a reason he was talking in depth about this very topic, just as I pulled in to the parking lot. Still infused with all the inspiring feelings I felt as I listened to Dr. Dyer's voice, I closed my eyes, took a deep breath, and said, "Thank you for guiding me to the book that will change the course of my life." I smiled as if I already had received what I asked for and walked into the bookstore. I looked around, feeling for any pull toward a particular section or book. I felt as if I was pulled toward Starbucks for a coffee and not anywhere else, so I obliged.

Then, as always after a cup of coffee, I was pulled to the bathroom. On my way back, I passed a book called *I Can See Clearly Now*. Since I resonated with the title, I knelt down to pull it from the shelf. I almost fell over when I saw that the book was written by Dr. Wayne Dyer, and it was the only book he'd ever written that told how he came to find his true calling. Shaking my head in disbelief, I somehow lifted my jaw off the floor and went to the register to make this book mine. I drove home, listening to *The Power of Intention* by

Dr. Dyer with a new understanding. It was as if he was sitting beside me in the car, speaking directly to me. I was so blown away by what had happened that I pulled over and "friended" him on Facebook.

The first post I saw of his on my timeline was "Did you ever feel like the universe is somehow conspiring for you?" In the comments, I told him about what had happened to me that day. He didn't reply, but many people did "like" my story. He and I were now in communication in the most indirect way.

I spent the next few days doing little else but reading his book. With every word, every page, every chapter I felt like he was telling my life story. I had knowledge, which kept growing in intensity, that his story was meant not only to explain the background of where his knowledge was coming from but for something bigger than that. On the evening when I finished the book, I went to check my inbox and found a promotional e-mail from a self-help guru named Brendon Burchard. I had been listening to his YouTube channel in the car on my way to see merchants. His videos were very inspiring and informational. His explanations of the way successful people think was of enormous help to me. His promotion for the book titled *The Millionaire Messenger* really got my attention. The premise was to help people share their life stories and knowledge with others, to help others overcome a difficult situation that they themselves were once a victim of.

The promotional video for the book explained that people are more receptive of people to whom they can relate. Sharing experiences with others unites us and brings us closer together. Living your life by helping, uplifting, and inspiring others to live their best lives is an actual career. Why did I believe him? I'd spent thousands of dollars buying audio books, online courses, and paperbacks to learn from others. I read *The Millionaire Messenger* and began to think about how I could build a career from this very new idea I had. I bought numerous other programs and dug deeper into the self-help world into which I'd first been pulled as a seeker and now as an advisor. I spent every day, morning to night, watching webinars and videos about this topic. If I had to leave the house, I listened to self-help business information on audio books. The more I dug deeper, the more I kept finding people who were living in service to others and making money—great money—while they were at it. I was filled with enormous amounts of information but I had not yet deciphered it all. I took a little break and went on Facebook to kill some time. Within seconds, I came across a video recorded by Ted McGrath, an inspiring leader in the field of self-help.

In it, he said, "You have to help others with your story. Think of the families that are counting on you. Think of all the people who guided you. Imagine they were too scared to share their voice. When you wander in the depth of your soul, wondering how it is going to work out, your soul already knows. It's written in your destiny. You just have to step in and trust. This is your calling. It's a new era. A new time is coming where we must lift each other up. We must share our experiences to create a change in other people's lives."

I watched that video over and over again, letting the words seep into my soul. I watched it every day with the clear understanding that it was meant for me. It was the sign I had been asking for, and it finally was staring me in the face. I was going to share my story, and I was going to do it by writing a book.

I had no idea how I was going to do it or what the structure of it would be. I just knew that this was the path for which I was destined. I finally had created my own dream on my own terms, just like the CEO of Lyoness had created his dream on his own terms. He had the right to do whatever he wanted. He had the balls to step in and share his vision, which is such a rare occurrence. I wasn't angry at him for changing the structure of the company; I understood him. He could pull the plug whenever he wanted. That was a privilege afforded only to those who have the courage to share their dreams and inspire others to dream with them. But the master who runs the show is the dreamer; he's the person who conceived the idea and set the intention.

This concept was very attractive to me. It made sense, and it began to build courage within me that I didn't know existed. I watched hundreds of videos about getting over fear—fear of sharing the truth about who you really are, about what really happens behind your smile, about what goes on in the bedroom when the front doors close. The real truth about my thoughts, struggles, and perceptions with zero care about how others would perceive me. I went from putting sparkles on everything, making it appear perfect—because that's what I was taught in sales—to getting real and raw, without losing my truth, solely to protect my image.

My image was my baby, and I would go to great lengths to protect it. Then one day I came across a video of a woman asking listeners to draw their lives as they were today. I drew a picture of myself behind bars, and out of my mouth was a voice box that was directed toward an image of our planet. Then she said, "Draw how you want your life to be in exactly one year from now, without giving it thought. Just draw." I drew myself without jail bars but still with a voice box directed to the world, only this time the world's voice box said, "Thank you." I looked at the drawing and realized that this was what I had wanted to do all my life. The vision of me being on stage to inspire others was not because I'd achieved a high level of commissions; it was because I wanted so badly to speak to massive groups of people. I wanted to share what I'd learned, how I felt, and my experiences, which if held within me would have all happened in vain.

If I shared my experiences, they would have a greater purpose, serving many more than just myself. My pain and struggle to figure things out might help those who were going through similar pain and struggle. When I began to share my ideas with others, every person said it was the perfect career move for me. As I shared bits and pieces of my deepest, darkest thoughts by blogging, my inbox would fill with people thanking me for being brave enough to share. Not one person thought my idea was crazy or that I was foolish to think I could serve others. It was time, however, to address my biggest fears, my biggest reasons for sabotaging myself.

I decided to splurge on a program that helps people deal with the underlying reasons for self-sabotage and why we constantly find a way to hold ourselves back. I was tired of constantly slowing myself down, and I needed to finally understand why I was a master at self-sabotage. In the video, the speaker, Ted McGrath, asked me to close my eyes. (I want to invite you to do the same exercise. You will find it very beneficial, as so many others have.)

"Go to your happy place," he said. "Feel the feelings of being there. Listen for the sounds that make this place so relaxing. Look around you and be present. Then, while your basking in your peace, ask for your higher self to come sit with you. Who is she? What is she wearing? What accomplishments is she celebrating? What is her annual income? Why is she smiling so brightly?"

As I sat in my happy place—my backyard at sunset—I felt the warmth of the sun kiss me. The air was still, and the colors in the sky changed from orange to pink right before my eyes. Then, I saw "Katerina" come outside to meet me. She was in the best shape of her life. She was wearing a body-hugging black dress and stunning black Louboutin heels. She'd just come back from celebrating her sixth week on the *New York Times* best-seller list. Her kids were so proud of her, and her husband was in awe of her incredible achievement. She was my higher self. She was me but not yet realized or manifested.

The voice on the video went on. "As you sit there with your higher self, ask her any question you want."

In my visualization, I turned to "Katerina" and asked, "How do I overcome my fear of putting my life out there? How do I get to be like you? How do I stop trying to figure out a distinct plan for how it will all work out? It's the lack of a plan that's stopping me from pursing my dream."

Within seconds, to my disbelief, I actually received a clear answer. "Katerina" said, "Don't worry about the details. Just start writing your heart out. It's all going to be worth it. Everything will somehow work out for you. Don't have any fear. I'll be here with you along the way. It's done. All you have to do is step in, and I'll take care of the details."

I felt so at ease. My biggest fear was that I didn't have a clear plan on how it would happen for me. I am a planner and a detail-oriented person. I plan my days for weeks and months in advance. But because this information was actually coming from "me" (the me I aspire to be), I didn't have any resistance against her advice. She knew me very well, so I didn't have the excuse of "She just doesn't get me." I felt as if I had seen the future and was assured that it was going to somehow workout. All I had to do was start. I thought back on how many thousands of opportunities worked out perfectly at a time when I'd least planned for and least expected them.

Surely if it happened thousands of times before throughout my life, it could happen again.

I went back to *The Secret* laws: Ask, Believe, Receive. This exercise was my introduction to believing in myself wholly. It didn't matter if I was talented enough to be an effective author. What mattered was that I desired to share my voice. I always held myself back if I wasn't able to be perfect at something. This time, the desire to be perfect was not going to stop me. True intention behind a dream is what makes the dream manifest. This is why it always baffled me why street musicians were sometimes better than musicians at sold-out concerts. I realized that the law of attraction does not discriminate. Surely this is the reason why so many of today's celebrities are not necessarily more talented than those in local theaters or street singers. It's all about the way you see yourself, not necessarily how you think the world perceives you or how you really are. Talent is one thing, but believing, seeing, and feeling yourself as talented is a lot more powerful. Feeling as if you are worthy of charging money for sharing your gift is the single biggest thing that separates successful people from the not-so-successful. That's it; that's all there is to it. This also explains how so many people came from nothing to become something on a massive global scale. Not all dreamers accomplish their dreams because of their opportunities; they do so because they believed opportunities would manifest someway, somehow. They just attracted events, people, and circumstances that helped them achieve their dreams and visions. It's as if by magic or luck that people went from living out of their cars to being on the Fortune 500 list. This became so clear to me that I felt I'd been given a free pass to overcome my fear … but I still had work to do.

One day I watched a webinar that was a huge game-changer for me. The speaker leaned toward the camera and loudly said, "You have all this knowledge, all these experiences you grew from, and you are going to be so selfish that you are going to keep them to yourself, just because you can't get over your fear. If you desire to help others, then help them. If you desire to preserve your image or not experience any negative feedback, then you are not made for this business. Here, in the self-help world, we help others. We don't hold back any information. It's not about you; it's about the families, the people who are counting on you to be brave, to share, and to create a shift within them."

Once I heard those words, I realized it wasn't about me or my fears. It was about serving people. It was about helping others overcome the horrors I'd lived through. From that moment on, I poured my heart out by blogging regularly. I created a Facebook page, "Happiest Mom on the Block," where I shared pictures of my life and my kids and expressed my deepest thoughts. Sometimes I don't resonate with many people, but when I do, the outpouring of gratitude I get is overwhelming. My inbox is always filled with messages from people I never met, thanking me for sharing my world.

That gorgeous spring day in 2015 was the day the first day I opened my computer and began to write the first few sentences of this book. As I sat in my bedroom with my laptop on my thighs, the words seemed to flow from my heart, right onto the computer screen. With each sentence, I was diving deeper within myself than ever before. Memories I suppressed and had not thought about were playing out in my mind as if I was right there, living them again. The pain of reliving some of the hardest moments of my life was very therapeutic and shifted to feelings of joy and closure. The hardest aspect was sharing my deepest secrets—potentially with the world. When I wrote, I was the real me—the one I'd tried so hard not to be because of my fear that I might be seen in a negative light. I was in my bliss; I was in a happy place. I was doing what I always knew I wanted to do, and to my shock, it was easier than I ever imagined. I'd spent years planning to write a book, constantly thinking of ways I would word certain events. Now, I was actually doing it. The biggest epiphany I had was that inaction is a lot more anxiety-ridden than the action itself. I was now free to follow my heart's desire to write without needing a plan on how it would work out. I just trusted that it would.

My whole being changed. I felt like I was looking at the world through eyes that focused on the perfection all around me. The girls now asked to go to sleep in their beds, and so we changed our nighttime rituals. Every night when I would put the girls to sleep, we would talk about being grateful and how wonderful it felt to say thank you for even the smallest gifts. One night, while we were doing our thank-yous, Milana started off by saying, "Thank you for making a yummy dinner. Thank you for wiping my tushy. Thank you to the star that shines so bright outside my window." Moments like these ignite so much joy within me.

I said, "Thank you for being so good to Mommy. Thank you for finishing your dinner and inspiring Madelyn to do the same. Thank you for your love." Madelyn could barely speak but she wanted us to go on with our thank-yous. It was as if it was a story for her. I could feel them being consumed with the light one feels when one's heart is focused on love and giving. My biggest prayer was that they would hold these memories dear to their hearts, always knowing that if they put themselves in a state of gratitude, they could feel the light of the universe shine within them.

When I first decided to put the girls in their beds, it was such a long process. They wanted to talk forever, and all I wanted to do was get them to sleep. Then, when I changed my thinking and began using this time to bond with them, I couldn't wait to get them in bed so that we could spend time together, talking about love and the beauty of the world. I always made sure to thank them for being so good and kind to each other and especially to me. I wanted them to know how much joy they brought to me, and so I always thanked them for making me so happy and proud.

It's a wonderful feeling to be appreciated for simply being yourself. The more I thanked them for being good, the better behaved they were. I noticed that they would go out of their way to be the best they could be almost all the time. Someone gave me the best advice when I was pregnant with Madelyn: spend your days making lists of all the things you want to praise your children for, and your lists of things to praise them for will grow. In my experience, this is 100 percent true!

Amazingly, there is a star outside the girls' bedroom window that shines brightly; it's like nothing I had ever seen. Milana referred to it as the Juliana star, and the tradition of wishing on stars was born. We felt like it was a wishing star because anything we wished for almost always came true. One night, Milana asked me what I wished for when I was a little girl.

I hugged her close and said, "I wished for this exact moment. I wished for you and your sister. I wished for Daddy and your brother. I wished for the life we live now." She was so excited to know that wishing on stars does work. She truly believed that anything could happen if you just feel the freedom to wish.

Wishing on stars is also a great way to teach children to think about their dreams before they go to bed. There was something so beautiful about listening to a five-year-old's wish. Often, it was, "I wish Mommy wouldn't get sick and would be with me for a long time," or "I wish Mommy has more babies so we can have more brothers and sisters," or "I wish to have powers so that I can make magic." It was a beautiful insight into her world and her thoughts. I wrote all our wishes and magical moments in a journal that I began writing when I found out I was pregnant with her.

I received a beautiful journal for Christmas 2007 from my mother-in-law. I had no idea what to use it for, so I threw it in the back of a drawer. One day, when I was a few weeks pregnant with Milana, I had the urge to write down my emotions. It was such an overwhelming time for me, but I had no one to share with, since my feelings and thoughts were intended for the baby growing inside me. I poured my heart out to her and couldn't wait until the day she read that letter. The first entry was when I was twelve weeks pregnant. I wrote about my dream when Juliana kissed my belly, and I felt a heart beating through my body. Every time I had a beautiful moment I wanted to share with her, I would write it down. When she was born, I wrote to her all the beautiful moments we shared. The writings were in letter form, and it felt so good to share with her all the emotions I was feeling at the time. I did this for Madelyn as well and later for Mason. Today, I have books of these letters for all my children. They are simple, cheap, and pretty journals, but they hold within them the most precious moments of my life and of my children's childhoods. I plan on writing as I always have and will give the books to them on their sixteenth birthdays, a time when most teenagers begin to rattle their relationships with their parents.

I also feel that if I share these magical moments with them— their first words, their funny sayings, their acts of unexpected kindness, and our nightly wishes on stars—surely it will give them a full understanding of how deeply loved they are. If something were to happen to me and I didn't live to tell them of the magic we shared, the healing I received from them, the privilege I feel of being blessed with motherhood, how lucky I consider myself to have children like them, how much I admire them, how much joy they give me, at least they will have my thoughts and memoirs to read. I want them to know how much I adore them, how much love we share every day, and what a gift they are to me and to the world. By reading the entries, we can forever relive the magnificent, awe-inspiring moments of their childhood. I realized that my emotions changed through every phase of their lives. When they were babies, I felt a peaceful, euphoric love for them. As they got older, my emotions were still infused with love, but there also was respect and admiration for the manifestation of their souls' true beauty.

We remember moments, but we often forget feelings, as they morph over the years. It was the feelings I wanted to share with them; they were so precious to me. I can die knowing they will know the truth of how I felt and never wonder about the depth of my love, joy, and gratitude that I was blessed with the privilege of bringing these beautiful souls into the world.

One of my biggest experiments was to rule the house by focusing on my own energy. When I was at peace, the children were peaceful. When I was frustrated with a circumstance, the children also would act in frustration. One day I noticed it so clearly that I put all my focus on being mindful of my energy. The calmer I was about asking them to do things, the more calmly they reacted to my requests. The biggest change happened when I decided that I would put them to sleep in their beds. Going to sleep with them at 9:00 p.m. no longer served me. I needed more time in the evening to do my writing and complete more self-mastery classes. I still welcomed them to my bed in the middle of the night if they needed a snuggle, but I was set on them falling asleep in their rooms. Once I truly and wholeheartedly decided on this, the children responded without hesitation. For many months I assumed they would never listen or want to go to bed, and guess what? They did exactly what I assumed they would do. They ran around until I gave in, ultimately falling asleep with them in their bed. The more I focused on believing that they would go to their own beds, the more they began to love falling asleep on their own.

Once you decide exactly what you want, and you have no doubt that your children will follow your desire, they actually do. It's the doubtful and fearful energy I used to emit that kept screwing me. Kids are not like adults; they are still raw. Their auras are still very open to receiving information from the energies around them. Once you master yourself, you master your children and their behavior. Someone once told me to discipline myself, not my children. These days, I expect my children to listen and to respect the few boundaries I set for them. I expect them to be the best they can be, and it's this expectation that drives them to be exactly what I expect them to be. There is no yelling or long explanations; there is rarely any need for compromise. They do the right thing almost all of the time.

I control everything in my life by controlling my energy, and controlling my children is just an extension of that concept. When I say *controlling* my children I don't mean running a strict household, where no one can express dislike for something. I am very open to the feedback I get from my kids. I have an enormous amount of respect for them. I control the energy in our house and use it as an invisible force to alter how my children behave and feel. This idea came to me when I noticed my inner feelings and actions changed when I was around different people. When I was in school, there were teachers who were able to control an unruly class with ease and a smile. Those teachers had students who were eager to listen and were on their best behavior. It was those teachers who were able to ignite an interest in a particular subject that was once of little interest to the students. It was as if the teacher's energy forced the students to put their guard down and open their minds to learn with excitement. Often, these teachers had students with the highest grades. It seemed that the behavior and emotional state of the students were almost fully dependent on the teacher. The strictest teachers had orderly classrooms, but most students lacked interest and were controlled from a place of fear, not an innate desire to be their best. Many of the unreasonably strict teachers had classrooms filled with students who were failing, even though they excelled in all other subjects. Other teachers, who seemed to struggle in life, were disorganized and lacked interest in their jobs. The more I thought about this concept, the more I realized how a parent's energy directly correlates with the behavior of her children. I experimented with this when I took the girls to a playground or the mall. Being alone with the two of them and pregnant in public places was a huge source of anxiety for me. I always assumed they would run away, I would lose one of them, or they would have an epic meltdown in the middle of the store. Because I was eight months pregnant, I knew I wouldn't be able to chase them around. I sat in the car in the mall parking lot and gathered my thoughts. I took a deep breath and said to myself, *I expect them to be on their best behavior. They will listen and stay near me at all times. They will be their very best, as they always are.* I took about five more deep breaths after I assured myself that all would be well. My energy was calm, and I was sure that the girls would not cause any havoc. I smiled at them and said, "Girls, thank you so much for coming with me to the mall. I can't wait to go in and show everyone how wonderful you girls are."

They both smiled, and I sensed them being proud of themselves for something I assumed they would do. To my shock, they were absolutely amazing that day. They didn't run away; they didn't make a mess; they held hands as we walked through the stores to pick up the things we needed. It was such a wonderful experience that I didn't have to say a word to them, other than "You girls are just so awesome. Thank you for making Mommy so happy." I did this many times when we went to the park, the grocery store, and even at other people's houses. When I would noticed that their behavior was becoming unruly, before saying anything to them, I would take a deep breath and center myself. I found a direct correlation between my anxious thoughts and their anxious behavior. It was so simple that it almost was impossible to comprehend at first, but with practice it became the biggest game-changer. "Everything begins with me" is a phrase I say to myself when I feel overwhelmed with their behavior. We, as parents, are in full control of our children as long as we are in full control of our inner world.

When you are mindful of the thoughts that feed your energy, children and adults seem to magically change their behavior to suit you. For example, dinner time at our house used to be when the children somehow got the order to run around, play, and do anything but sit down and eat. The more they did this, the more I anticipated that they would do it. I almost expected them to do everything but eat. I would begin dinner by saying, "Come sit down and eat. Don't get up until you are done," but my expectation was that they wouldn't sit, so I emitted an energy that expected them not to eat. So, they did not eat but ran around, just as I expected them to.

I was shocked when I walked in to Madelyn's daycare during lunch one day and watched my two-year-old sit down and eat her meal without getting up. All the other children were sitting down as well, eating and not even fidgeting in their seats. I asked her daycare teacher how she accomplished this.

She smiled and asked, "Accomplished what?"

I said, "Get them to sit down to eat their lunch!"

She laughed. "Oh, they are expected and told to sit down to eat. Why would they get up?"

Her clear expectation drove them to do what she expected them to do. She didn't beg them, she didn't compromise with them, and she didn't make any excuses for them. She only expected them to do what she expected them to do.

The more time you spend expecting the best of your children and seeing their goodness, even on their "off" days, the more you will see them bringing forth the best of themselves.

One of the biggest changes I noticed was the disappearance of Madelyn's temper tantrums—she was then two years old. When I was pregnant, dealing with my hormones and the never-ending desire to get things done quickly and efficiently, I noticed that Madelyn was the first to fall apart. She seemed to be the most sensitive to my energy; she was the youngest and most receptive to the energy around her. When I noticed how my anxiety affected her, I was inspired to take control over myself.

At first it was hard. My raging pregnancy hormones had put me in an irritable state, and her crying on the floor would set me off. But the more frustrated I was, the worse her reaction was, which ultimately led to her hyperventilating and my needing to calm her down for a really long time. As soon as I saw that her face was beginning to lose its usual smile, I would do a breathing exercise and bring myself to a calm, happy state. I wasn't going to prevent a meltdown, but I was going to alleviate the severity of it. After I calmed my nerves, I was able to emit a soothing, happy frequency around myself. Instead of letting her crying escalate, I would pick her up so that she would be close to me. I would continue doing my breathing and visualize that she was receiving my calming, soothing energy. As I held her close, she often would first fight me, but I'd hold on to her and kept breathing. I would sing her favorite lullabies and take her by the window to show her something beautiful outside. With my voice soft and soothing, I would tell her stories of baby birds outside, of flowers blossoming, and of the clouds passing by. The longer I held her within my energy, the easier it was for me to distract her from her frustration. At first, it would take me a good fifteen minutes to calm her, but as I learned to bring myself to a state of peacefulness, my energy more quickly merged with hers. I was focused on showing her a positive reaction to her meltdown, and that reassured her that I loved her no matter how she was feeling. I showed her and Milana that my feelings were not controlled by Madelyn's crying or other circumstances. I was in control of my reactions; I would not lose it like a toddler loses control of her emotions and thus have a meltdown too. I was the adult. I was the center of energy, and they could rely on me for support.

The power of expectation—if you expect your children to go through the terrible twos, they absolutely will. If you expect your children to run around the mall, they will. If you expect your children to not listen, they absolutely won't. So many mothers say to me, "My kid is a troublemaker" or "My kid doesn't listen no matter what I do." Yes, if you assume your child is a troublemaker, he absolutely will live up to that label. If you assume your kids are bad listeners, they will prove you right. When someone says, "My kid is ____, no matter what I do," it's not that the child is un-disciplinable;

it's that the parent has given up on the idea that she can be in full control of her expectations.

Supernanny is successful in getting children to change their behavior because she comes into the house where she doesn't know the kids' behavioral problems. She has no knowledge of their past behavior, and she expects them to abide by the rules she sets; she has little reason to believe they won't. When she comes in with her positive, assured energy, somehow even the biggest problem child happily abides. The parents have seen their child at his worst, and so their expectation of his behavior continues to take a downward spiral. They feel hopeless and helpless—not a good combination of energy when you are trying to help a child find joy in being good for himself and his parents.

For a peaceful, happy home, a parent's wants and expectations of the child must be in sync and must be on the same feeling frequency.

As you spend time training yourself to expect the best of your children, the best of your children is what you will see!

There should be certain set of rules that are never to be broken, not by the child and not by the parent. Very clear guidelines must be laid out that all family members must live by. We have the big three: no disrespect, no speaking negatively, and show kindness. When I was growing up, I was taught that disrespect is disobedience. My understanding of respecting my elders and parents was simply obeying them. It was a black-and-white understanding. Do what you are told. If you go against what you are told, you are being disrespectful. If you do what you are told, you are being respectful.

There was one circumstance when I was fourteen, talking to a friend on the phone, and my dad picked up the extension and yelled, "Get off the phone! I need the phone!" I was upset, as my friend and I were in the middle of a very interesting conversation. I said, "Just give me a few minutes, and I'll hang up."

My dad insisted I was being disrespectful because I didn't hang up immediately. To me, however, I was respecting my and my friend's desire to finish our conversation. I wasn't hurting anyone. My dad didn't need to make an emergency call; he simply remembered to call someone and wanted to do it immediately. I often wondered why respect was considered a one-way street. Why were we considered disrespectful if we chose not to do what someone told us to do? What about respecting ourselves and our own desires? Wasn't that just as important?

Now that I am older, my understanding of respect is listening to another human being without judgment or argument and at the same time making my own decision. You don't actually have to obey to respect; you can treat a person with kindness while making your own choice. When I decided to make respect one of the unbreakable rules in my house, I had to be very clear with my children about what it meant.

Respect, in my view, means to be mindful of how personal actions impact others. At even the slightest attempt to show respect for anyone, I acknowledge how proud I am of the choice Milana made to be respectful. I give a high-five and say, "You always amaze me with how you treat others. Thank you for being such an inspiration to me." I always check myself to make sure I display respect for other people and especially our children. This rule was implemented in our home from the moment Milana was able to understand it, which was when she was around two and half. If you make it a rule to live by from a very young age, it becomes second nature to children, making it easier for you to enforce it as they get older.

I also find that disrespectful kids are often disrespected by their elders. If you teach a child respect by displaying it, you make yourself a better human being and set the expectation of your children's behavior toward others. All human beings are worthy of respect, regardless of their age, race, or place in society.

One of the biggest realizations I had was when I saw my friend's children disrespect her. They spoke to her in a derogatory way, almost exactly like her husband did. She allowed her husband to disrespect her, and her children treated her the same way. How can you expect respect from your children but not from your spouse?

If your husband says "shut up" to you, and you don't stop him by saying, "Never, ever speak that way to me," you give invisible permission to your children to treat you similarly.

Show your children the importance of respecting yourself by taking care of your temple, carefully selecting the food you allow into your body, watching the language you use toward yourself, and of course accepting only the best in your life. If you have a set expectation of how you want to be treated, you will be treated the way you expect. When James would speak negatively toward me, I did not always make a point of correcting his treatment because I didn't want to start anything. Almost always, the children's behavior would change toward me for the rest of the day, sometimes even longer. However, when you see yourself as someone who respects all and demands respect from all, you will establish a natural respectful behavior in your children.

If the rules are set in the household, everyone must abide by them. It's the only way to get results. You get what you expect, if you expect it frequently enough. Some elders say that kids are disrespectful these days because they don't get spanked enough. Adults may use physical force because they lost control over themselves; they lost the power and ability to control their anger. You can't "beat" respect into a child; you can only receive behavior that you yourself display. Treat your child with the utmost respect for their ideas, their voices, and their desires, and watch how quickly they reciprocate.

Chapter 11

Let's get scientific about how the child's brain works. From birth to about age six or seven, a child's brainwaves are very slow. The child functions from his subconscious mind. Everything you tell him he will perceive as true. He doesn't yet have the analytical ability to interpret information as right or wrong. All of children's awareness is in their internal environment. A child's brain has something called a mirror neuron; it's an empathy neuron, which means the child models what you do more than what you say.

For example, when you are feeding your baby, you may open your mouth as you put the spoon in, hoping the baby will do the same. And she often does open her mouth just like you did, mirroring your behavior.

When a lioness teaches her cubs how to hunt, she doesn't tell them what to do. She indicates, *stay here and watch me*. As your children watch what you are doing, they turn on the same circuits in their brains as if *they* were actually doing it. That primes the brain and molds the child's behaviors. If you have an issue with a child's behavior, look at yourself. Use this child's behavior as a red flag that the behavior you display and the behavior you expect may not be in sync. Address your issues first; then you can address your child's behavior. The idiom "the apple does not fall far from the tree" holds a lot of truth. Your children are your mirrors, at least for the first six or seven years of their lives.

You are the control center of their behavior. Once you are aware of it, you can change the way they act and think. Another important event that happens in the first five years of development is the building of children's belief system. This belief system will control most of the decisions they make in life. For example, how an adult sees money, relationships, and choice of career is often controlled by the information they received from their family in the first five years of life. Knowing this, be very careful of the type of belief systems you create for your children. It helps to examine your own belief systems so that you can pinpoint which ones you want to let go of and which ones you want to implement for your own children to use in adulthood.

I try to teach my kids that life is easy, problems are rare, and as long as they are doing what makes them happy, they will be successful. I want to set them up for a life of ease and a life of happiness. What you expect, you receive. I know that this belief system will serve them.

The second rule is no negative talk. We are a "yes" house. Using yes more frequently than no gives no significantly more power. I reserve the word no for very dire situations, so that when I do say it, it's like a shockwave in my children's brains. I also found that the more I use yes, the more they use yes.

When a child becomes mobile and aware of her hands, they have an insatiable desire to explore the world. From one to two years old, children hear no a lot more often than yes. After age two, they begin to model what they heard in the last year of their lives. That's why when you ask your two-year-old to put on her shoes, she often says no. When you ask your two-year-old to stop doing what she is doing, he often says no. Why? That's what he heard on a daily basis for an entire year. Before I say no, I always check myself to make sure it's a valid reason to use this word.

It seems the word *stop* is more powerful when it comes to preventing a dangerous act. If Milana was running toward the street, that would be a great time to use *stop* to stop her in her tracks. But when Milana is touching the TV or climbing up the stairs, I would rather stand by her to assist her if she needs me instead of using the word no. Because of the mirrored neurons in their brains, I was able to create "yes children"—most of the time anyway. I know how much power I have over them, and I use that power very sparingly. I want to be effective, not mundane. This was one the best choices I made when it came to parenting. Create a "yes house" by putting away valuables that might interest an exploring toddler. Put up gates so that you don't need to use *no* too frequently. Create a yes environment, where children can roam freely without harming themselves or lowering their desire to explore the world. When their home is a place they feel most free, they will satisfy their curiosity without causing havoc or feeling constricted. When a child doesn't feel free, he acts out as soon as he gets a little freedom. (I'm sure you know plenty of kids who come from strict households, and as soon as they leave their parents' house, they act in unusually crazy ways.) Plus, it makes your job easier if you're not always running around after them screaming, "No!"

Another part of the "no negative talk" rule is that I don't allow my kids to complain or say things like "I can't do it," "I hate that," or "That tastes disgusting." I know many people don't allow their kids to curse, and when they do, they say, "Watch your mouth." Luckily, for now, my kids don't find cursing appealing (even though I am guilty of it myself). But if they begin their sentences with something negative or are speaking poorly of another person, I remind them to *watch their mouths*. I believe that words that don't add to the positive energy around us cannot be of use to us.

When you utter words like hate or disgusting, you create a negative energy within yourself that only makes you feel worse. I want my children to focus on words that bring a positive light, not those words that rob their environment of that light. I speak very kindly to the girls, often respectfully using words like, "Would you be kind enough to bring me that?" I never used to speak that way. I am Russian and grew up in Brooklyn. Russians have a way of barking orders. It's not out of disrespect; it's just the way we speak. And the Brooklyn dialect is also not the most loving and kind either. My parents didn't speak this way to me, and I never understood the power of speaking kindly … until I met a woman a few years ago who changed my view on the power of language.

I was a few months pregnant with Milana, and this woman and I were both standing in line at the grocery store. She had her daughter with her, who was about five years old. The woman didn't want to purchase the cookies her daughter selected.

"Would you please be kind enough to put these back on the shelf? I don't think we need them. We have plenty at home. Thank you so much, sweetie. I really appreciate it." Her voice was so calm and serene, yet firm. She got her point across by using a beautiful bouquet of words to convey what she wanted from her daughter. Of course, her daughter didn't question her; she obliged without hesitation.

I was in shock; it made such a huge impact on me that I swore I would speak the same way to my friends and family and most certainly to my kids. It felt good to speak in a calm, respectful manner, using words that conveyed positive emotions. After a few years it became second nature to me. When I used a calm, soothing voice, everyone around me listened and did what I asked of them almost immediately. "Enjoy yourself, girls, and play as much as you want, but if you need something, would you please let me know?" That phrase almost guarantees the kids will be on their best behavior. It sets off such a positive energy that consumes everyone in the room.

When we are at the store, I am shocked when I hear parents say in an annoyed tone, "Don't touch anything. You can't have that. I said no." Those children are being dragged through the store where so many beautifully marketed items are displayed. Their desire is to explore, feel, and touch. Why speak to them so angrily? Why expect them to break things or to grab things? What if they just want to look? Imagine how those children feel, being spoken to like they are about to do something wrong. Why wouldn't they? They already feel punished and disrespected. Why not do whatever they want to do? Their mother is trying to do some shopping and get out; I understand her. But there is a kinder way of treating children in such interesting places as the grocery store or the mall. Sadly, those children often turn out to be just as rude to their parents as their parents are to them. It's so much nicer to speak kindly to children and all human beings. It makes the world a nicer place to live when kindness is felt in the heart and expressed through words.

I also found that my assumption of the child's response determines the tone I use. When I expect the kids to respond negatively, my voice when speaking to them is abrasive. When I expect a positive response from my children, my voice is kind and gentle. I expect my children to be on their best behavior when we are out shopping, and so my tone is respectful. "Isn't this store amazing? So many things to look at. Enjoy looking, but please keep in mind that Mommy has a limited amount of time to get the grocery shopping done." But if I expect the kids to touch, play, and run around the store, my tone and choice of words would be something like, "Don't touch anything. I don't have time. We need to get the groceries and get out, so don't give me a hard time." Of course, the kids can feel my negative expectation of them, and often that is exactly what they do.

Expect your children to be their best when you speak to them, and you will see them meet your highest expectations.

So the next time you hear your kids speaking negatively or venting, stop them and remind them to watch their mouths, and divert their attention to something wonderful that ignites a positive emotion within them. Begin the hard work of watching your own mouth, and the incredible impact you make on your children will astonish you.

The third rule that is unbreakable in our house is that we must be kind, and that includes not being stingy. I often remind my children that we have been blessed with so much, and there is nothing we can't replace. James's grandmother taught me a beautiful lesson. The easiest way to teach kids the importance of human emotion over material things is to remind them, *People before things*. If there is something in your home that is of irreplaceable value, put it away for now. You'll have plenty of time to marvel at it when the children get older. Your home should be a place that is inquisitive-child-friendly, not a display of incredibly valuable goods. When the girls are arguing over a toy, I remind them to put each other before the toy. It's more important to show kindness and share than having the toy. When the girls break something in the house that's valuable, they often get scared and feel remorseful for the accident. I calmly remind myself out loud, "People before things." The more I do this, the more they understand that I value them much more than I value the material object.

I also try to model behavior that is kind and welcoming to everyone who comes to our home. I always speak out loud as I am cooking or preparing gifts for others. "I can't wait for everyone to come over so they can enjoy these wonderful yummies I bought." During Christmas, I wrap gifts with the children, saying, "How wonderful is this gift? I really hope it makes her happy. I am so glad I was able to find it. It's perfect." Since I began to focus in on kindness, I am proud of Milana when she gives away a toy to every friend that comes to our house. It's so beautiful to watch her go through her toy box and pick out the perfect toy she would love her friend to have. I love seeing her light up with joy when she gives from an open heart. I assure them that we have and can get all the toys in the world, alleviating the feeling of not having enough. There's no need to fuss over a toy that her sister, the person she loves so much, wants to play with. The more Milana shares, the more easily Madelyn shares. If there is a toy that I know Milana is busy playing with, then that toy is off limits. It took a while for me to teach Madelyn that Milana really loves playing with her doll and that she is in the middle of a game.

"Let's let Milana finish her game. She is such a good sister to you. Let's find a doll that looks almost like the one Milana is playing with."

Even though Madelyn can sometimes be upset, it's very short-lived because Milana will almost always find a way to include Madelyn in the game. Milana felt the respect I had for her game, and there was no resistance to feel against her sister or me. It's all about opening up energy within the child and eliminating reasons to create resistance.

Due to the openness and receptive nature of children, you can mold them into anything you want them to be ... as long as what you want them to be is in direct accordance with the basic nature of positive human emotion. It is more natural to be happy than miserable. It's more natural to be kind than stingy. It's more natural to be on your best behavior than act out in anger or have complete disregard for those you love (e.g., parent, sibling, or friend). Teach children (and yourself) to focus on living from the heart rather than the ego. Be the person you want your children to be, and watch your entire family dynamic change. Children, like adults, are always looking for heroes, someone to look up to, someone they can trust to lead the way for them. If you can accommodate this need for them, your children will treat you like the hero you are.

I put away all the parenting books and began to explore the world of leadership, learning about successful leaders who are so extraordinary that people naturally follow them. A great leader does not lead with force but with a kind, gentle, positive assumption that he is doing what's best for the people. A great leader rarely falls apart when things don't go her way. He doesn't take things personally and is able to offer solutions rather than find problems. A great leader will always find a way to put people on a pedestal and lead from a place of adoration, rather than from a place of dismay for those who are following her. A great leader leads with his mission statement. What is your mission statement when it comes to how you want your household to be?

Ours is "Always do what feels good to you" and "Kindness and

159

love for everyone on the planet always wins." I sometimes get a lot of heat for teaching my kids that they should be kind to everyone in the world because the world is filled with bad people. Yes, the world does have some really bad people, but it's not my job to teach my kids about that. My job is to maintain their expectation that all people of the world deserve to be loved, to experience an act of kindness, and to have their feelings considered. Bad people are "bad" because they are hurting. They are missing something essential in their lives; often, they are missing love. Explaining this to my children teaches them compassion rather than judgment of others for their choices. It seems that as soon as pure, innocent children are of age, the parents teach them about all the bad things that can happen to them or in the world. Parents feel they are protecting their children, but in reality they are skewing their children's experiences. Children have the right to experience life for themselves through their own eyes. We get from others what we give. It has nothing to do with good or bad people.

Understanding that your assumptions and beliefs rule your universe and experiences, what if the assumptions and beliefs were that of a positive world? Wouldn't that, through the law of attraction, attract a world that is indeed magnificent and filled with loving, caring people? I am not perfect, nor do I expect my kids to be. I do make mistakes and sometimes the smaller part of me takes over the bigger part of me. Sometimes I lose it, and sometimes I yell. Sometimes my kids witness an argument between James and me that embarrasses me. Sometimes I am not my best self. Sometimes I express anger because that is what I feel. But I don't focus on my mistakes. I focus on the ways I am my best self.

What you focus on grows and becomes a part of you. Focus on the best of your mothering abilities, and let go of guilt when you mess up. It not only teaches your kids that humans mess up, even Mom, but it also teaches them to recover quickly from a negative situation so that their best selves are able to shine through. Guilt blocks your best self from emerging and dominating your existence.

After you have a day when you lose it, say sorry to everyone you affected, and explain that you are human; it happens. As soon as you do that, focus all your attention on being your very best.

When I began my own journey of self-discovery, one of my biggest mental blocks came from being brought up by a worrier. A worrier is someone who, from a place of love, worries about everything the child—and later, the adult—does. Something as innocent as "Don't do that. You're going to crack your head open," or "Don't run. You're going to fall" comes from a place of concern and caring for the child. In my case, I always heard "Don't do this … because this might be the outcome." Though the chances of my falling if I ran too fast were real, the chance was small. The amazing sensation of running fast beat the small chance of my falling. And so what if I fell? I'd get up. If banged myself up, I'd heal. The feeling of freedom that came from running run as fast as I could, however, more than made up for the pain.

As I was trying to figure out my dream, I kept giving myself millions of reasons why it might not work. I heard my mother's voice in my head: "Be careful. You might get hurt." Yes, when you pursue your dreams you might get hurt, but so what? Isn't the thrill of life worth the risk of doing something you feel deep within your heart and then basking in the glory of accomplishment? Isn't that what life is all about? Isn't that what everyone is seeking, or is it the safe nine-to-five job that pays the bills but doesn't keep the flame of passion lit? Surely there is another way to live your life, isn't there? Playing it safe is not liberating, and it's not where the true joy of life resides.

Think of every risk you ever took, including becoming a parent. It was scary at first, but when you finally got to raise your child, wasn't it the greatest, most gratifying risk ever? I always allow my kids to run around, to push themselves on the monkey bars, and really have fun playing, without me breathing down their backs, reminding them of what might go wrong. I want my children to feel my trust in them. My assumption is that they will not get hurt

161

and will persevere, contrary to what I see on the playgrounds these days. Parents assume that their kids will get hurt, and often they do.

Have you ever attempted something but felt the lack of support from a loved one? You get shaky, you start to question your abilities, and often you fail, not because you couldn't do it but because you didn't have your loved ones' faith in your abilities. The children feel that their parents don't believe in their ability to look out for themselves. Once they don't feel their parents' support, they lose balance, often falling harder than if they felt their parents' belief in their actions.

We have a fourteen-foot staircase in our house, Milana can't resist sliding down the railing. At first, I gasped as she slid down, telling her, "Oh, my God, get down. You're going to fall." But then, I stopped looking and told her, "You're on your own with this one. If you feel like you can handle it, go for it. But I don't agree with your going down the stairs in this manner, so if you fall, it's all on you."

After years of her doing this—and now Madelyn attempting it as well—not one fall has occurred, and I don't expect one anytime soon. My kids are so sure of themselves that they keep themselves safe. I am also afraid of losing credibility with them by telling them something might go wrong. When it doesn't, that takes away my ability to judge a situation in their eyes. Interestingly, children have an innate desire to keep themselves alive, and if given the chance, they can really impress you.

When Madelyn turned a year old, she began to climb the stairs. At first I thought I needed to put up a gate to protect her, but then I asked Milana to teach her the proper way of going up and down the stairs. Amazingly, she learned to skid down and never had a fall. What's the saying? Give a man a fish, and you feed him for a day; teach a man to fish, and you feed him for a lifetime. A similar saying can be applied to kids. Teach kids to safely explore their world while instilling the belief that they are trusted to watch out for themselves. You can calmly enjoy your children without worrying much about them if you fully trust them—assuming they are strong and able to care for themselves.

The only way to know their strengths is to allow them to roam freely. They often will surprise you with their abilities. When my kids are ready to pursue the journey of dreaming up their lives, they won't think of what might may go wrong; they will feel empowered to handle any situation that comes their way, especially mastering the art of falling, dusting themselves off, and moving forward.

It all comes down to the mother. If you feel that you are in control of your inner world, you won't feel compelled to control those around you. Allow your children to fall, to get up, and to follow their desires. Isn't getting up after a fall reassurance that you took a risk and you still survived? In life, weren't the most empowering moments and most character-building experiences when you failed but managed to get up and persevere on a level you never thought possible?

As a mother, I feel it is my duty to create an environment where my children can access and nourish their God-given gifts. Milana is quite the talker and is determined to get her thoughts across. Some say she "has a mouth on her" and jokingly call her "sassy," but to me, she is an open book. If I ask her to do something that she doesn't feel is right or necessary, she will explain why she doesn't agree with me. Sometimes it can be quite annoying to me, especially when I am not in the mood to analyze a situation and just want to get things done. Many refer to such children as strong-willed or even stubborn. I don't know why we need to label kids who feel the freedom to openly express themselves when they don't agree with what someone says. When I do get frustrated, I remind myself that this attribute is the single biggest reason why she won't be bullied in school or later in life by an employer or the man with whom she has a relationship. I can deal with her need to do what she feels is right, even if I don't agree. She isn't being disrespectful; she is being respectful of her God-given intuition and desire so speak up for what she feels isn't right for her. For this girl, my saying "because I said so" just wouldn't suffice as a reasonable explanation. It's my job as a parent to provide an environment where freedom to express oneself is acceptable and encouraged.

I have always wondered how our souls are born into bodies. How we can have a few minutes of lovemaking, and with a little bit of luck we create a perfectly functioning human being? How does this happen? Have you ever wondered where souls come from? I have an explanation that may sound very "out there," but it resonates with me; maybe it will with you as well. Humans being are born with souls. They are pure, positive energy. They are all that they are without being molded just yet. Babies spend most of their time sleeping, and the gap between sleeping and their conscious and awake world is closed. Then they wake up and the gap widens. As babies grows into toddlers, they learn the ways of being human. They have experiences throughout life from which they learn and grow. All the information that is learned throughout a lifetime is stored within a human being's soul. Then the human being dies. All that information is the vantage point from which they will begin when they choose the next set of parents for themselves; that is, when they decide to return to earth for another human experience. They will reincarnate with the same soul, packed with information learned in previous lifetimes, but into a different genetic line. This is where the saying "old soul" comes from. It's used so widely when parents gaze at their children's eyes, and they seem so deep; the children seem to have knowledge of what life is all about. That is because they do; they are old souls. They have reincarnated, carrying information throughout their lifetimes.

This is why the TV program *20/20* loves to do shows on kids who are three years old and can play the piano better than an experienced music teacher; why some four-year-olds understand the concept of God better than grown adults; why a seven-year-old can come on a talent show and sing like she has the voice of a professional adult singer, sending chills down our spines as we watch in awe; and why my six-year-old explained to me that in order to go to heaven you don't need a body. You just need a body to be here on earth so you can learn about why you're here.

So let's agree that souls do travel from body to body, carrying vital information. This can also explain why our babies can master technology better and faster than our parents or us. Their vantage point has evolved. This is also why every time human beings are born, they don't learn everything they know. They just have a *knowing* of some things. I call it the gut instinct or intuition.

Recently, the president of Autism Autoimmunity Project confirmed that there has been an 800 percent increase in autistic children since the 1980s. More younger kids are coming out as gay or lesbian than ever before. There are more kids born with extraordinary abilities to fight the norm. These new energies are coming to earth, and they are so strong that they refuse to conform in any way. They seem to question everything that they don't understand. They have such a strong sense of purpose that they won't listen to authority and will question everything and everyone, not out of distrust but out of trusting their own intuition. It doesn't seem right to them, even at very young ages.

Recently I have focused on teaching my kids to do what they *feel* is right, not do what they *think* is right. When they live in their heads, they make logical assumptions and find logical solutions to problems. Sometimes they're right; sometimes they're wrong. But if they live in their hearts—if they live from a place of feeling situations out—they can't go wrong. How many times in your life has your intuition been wrong? How many times in your life has your logical mind been wrong? Intuitive decisions are always the right ones, even if they seem wrong or illogical at first. No matter how wrong you want your intuition to be, it's always right.

Today, parents are researching how to handle their strong-willed children more than any other topic related to parenting. It seems these new, powerful, extraordinary kids (as I call them, Generation X-traordinary) are coming here to facilitate change in the world. Very little change can happen with forces that are easily molded or that conform to the norm. It's the people who refuse to conform to society or authority that bring about the biggest changes … and they have. There has been a massive influx of parents researching and implementing homeschooling, more than ever before in our modern world. The National Center for Educational Statistics of the United States Department of Education reported that in 1999, there were 850,000 children educated at home. In 2012 there were 1.77 million children educated at home, a 108 percent increase in just thirteen years. There is no doubt that this number will continue to grow as more resources and information is available to parents.

Parents are realizing that their children are unusually bright but are unable to conform to school policy or rules. Many of these children, particularly those carrying the labels of ADHD and autistic, are unable to sit in a classroom with other children. How can they? They are born different with a different sense of reality. This is not to say that their reality is off; it is just different. Doctors and parents of autistic children agree that the children are unusually bright; they are just not conforming to what we know as "normal" behavior. What is a "normal" child? Is it a child who is like his mother's friend's child? Where are we getting the comparisons? All children are born normal when you take away the label and expectation of the term "normal." Maybe the ADHD children and autistic children are driving the change within the school system. Maybe that is their purpose for being here—to teach us to make changes—and with the support of their parents, they have *facilitated change*! Almost every school has a special-needs program for these children. When I was in school during the 1990s, special programs were mainly for disabled children, not for "special learners." We must understand that this group of kids is not to be judged but understood. They are not to be molded but allowed to blossom on their terms and their beliefs within their reality. Every child is born special, engraved with special gifts that are unique to him or her. If you have a child who does not meet the criteria of "normal," don't feel forsaken.

Our children chose us as their parents and come here to teach us something about the world or ourselves. Most parents with ADHD or autistic children demand information from the medical community. These parents have been at the forefront of demanding that food companies eliminate toxic ingredients, poisonous preservatives, and genetically modified ingredients and have brought to light the importance of farmers who choose to grow their food without the use of pesticides and in clean soil. (This has led to the explosion of knowledge about organic food.) These parents are the ones who have fought with the school systems, demanding a change in classroom settings and teachers who are specifically trained to teach these "special learners." These parents have shaken up the entire medical community and questioned vaccines and the side effects of mercury.

These new energies coming in have a very clear understanding of their purpose, and it's our job to create environments in which we drown them in unconditional love, compassion, and acceptance so that they can bloom to be who they really are, not who we, doctors, or therapists think they should be. No amount of medication can help a child who is struggling to adjust to our world. Modern medicine and psychology can't take the place of parental love and acceptance. You can medicate a child for a temporary effect, but the most profound impact you can make on a child is unconditional acceptance, unconditional love, and unconditional care. Nourishing foods and nourishing environments may seem like a huge responsibility to take on, but I believe that it's essential to allowing our children to become all that they are born to be.

The day I stopped questioning why my daughter was born with cancer and began to seek her purpose in choosing me as her mother was the day I began to fully live. I believe Juliana chose me to ignite in me a fire for seeking truth and an understanding of the universe but certainly not to forsake or burden me. Because of her terminal diagnosis I was compelled to learn about food, the environment, and how I could live the healthiest life possible. Her death ignited within me a knowing that there are other dimensions where our loved ones go after they are no longer in the physical realm. She also gave me such a deep understanding of the miracle that is our bodies. All of my children seem to have qualities within them that make them different from other children. They are unusually sensitive to changes, to a tone in my voice, and to demands that seem to have no clear reasoning. I realize that the world is changing rapidly and absolutely for the better. People are gathering to stand up for human rights and animal rights like never before.

In 2013 *Time* magazine made "the Protester" the person of the year, supporting my understanding that people are fighting against oppression and are demanding change within our society. People understand that the world is not intended to be a place of struggle and accepting the norm; it's a place where you have your own voice, if you cultivate it enough.

I always try to raise my children to be the best version of themselves and to learn and explore themselves, their desires, and their needs. (This is something I wasn't taught as a child and only began to explore when I was in my thirties.) I want them to have a sense of self-worth with which they are well acquainted and are as close to their intuition as they can be. I want them to feel things out and, if they don't feel right, to trust in that feeling, even if it means disregarding logic.

Many studies are being blogged about that refer to this new generation as the worst in math and one that struggles with memory problems. They blame technology, and they are right to do so. This new generation could not care less about logic (math); they are all trying to feel things out, using their intuition and discovering their "knowing." They have access to more information than any previous generation, thanks to Google, bloggers, and YouTube. They don't feel they need to store all the information they read; they know it's there for them if they need it, right at their fingertips. They are amazing researchers, and if they have any questions, they don't go to their parents; they go to the world online, where everyone seems to be sharing their experiences, struggles, and breakthroughs.

Their guidance is not limited to their parents or schoolbooks; they are connected to the entire world and all of its experiences. How amazing is that?

Another aspect of this new generation is that they are able to connect with people from all walks of life, eliminating the need to label others or have any prejudice. When they research a topic—online, for example—they receive information, and if it resonates with them, they accept it, though they have no idea what race, religion, or country the particular person is from who provided the information. This is what leads me to believe that this generation will be the most open-minded, most informed generation of our time.

Milana, at age five, explained something to me that left me speechless. She said that a person's color is determined by the amount of sun their ancestors had in the particular region they are from. The darker the skin, the more sun their country of origin had. The lighter-skinned people had less sun. Oh, my God! This is it? That is all that skin color represents? Why didn't I ever think of that? Oh, maybe because our parents' generation was taught separation rather than unity. Though I am so grateful to be an '80s–'90s child, growing up during times where racism began its final descent from acceptable behavior. This new generation, if allowed to blossom, will never experience the horrors of human slavery, racism based on skin color, or the incredibly tragedy of the extermination of Jews during the Holocaust. They are not group thinkers; they are individuals who must be praised for their beliefs. If we all consciously agree to make an effort to support this new generation, rather than trying to make them conform, imagine the change we could see and experience in the world!

There is more to our children than just little bodies eager to learn. They are also eager to teach us something we may be missing or may have forgotten. Children have a clear understanding of why we have the gift of life. They are not yet busy with life's demands, as adults are. Their purpose in life is centered on feeling joy and unconditional love at all times. Just look at the way children spend their days; it's all about exploring, learning, laughing, and giving their parents unconditional love. Children are born with the desire to love all that exists and don't yet have the ability to judge something by its color, appearance, or difference from their own beliefs. They do not yet have beliefs, just observations. They have not yet been tarnished by life experiences that often skew our mind-set rather than allow it to grow. So many adults are plagued by their life experiences. If humans see a snake in the forest, for the rest of their lives, every time they walk through a forest, instead of enjoying the scenery they look down, making sure there is no snake on the path! Children don't have any life experience that shapes their understanding of the world. They are still able to see infinite possibilities within all their dreams and desires.

Maybe we can learn a thing or two from them if we just take off our "I'll teach you because I know a thing or two about life" hats and use our children to remind us of what we may have forgotten. Why do we have so much fun on the weekend when we hang out with our kids and then dread Monday and going back to work? Maybe it's because it feels so good to be around their pure energies, and it feels so bad to be around adults' beat-up, low energies at work. Maybe it's because having fun with our kids brings us closer to our true nature. Maybe if we were always allowed to be who we really are, to be one with our inner voices, we would never make choices that would get us into jobs solely to pay the bills. (I recently saw a meme that read "JOB—Just Over Broke." I thought it was pretty accurate.)

After college we wouldn't take any job that would take us. We would consciously choose the job of our dreams. Or we would create an opportunity for ourselves with little fear of failure because we knew we were cultivating our gifts and our purpose. We would pursue our passions from a very young age, with a deep trust that it would all work out since it is our purpose for being here. It's a fact that those who pursue a life they are meant for have little worry about financial abundance. Doors seem to open in places where there once were walls for those who dare to dream and pursue a life of purpose. The main reason we don't pursue our dreams is because somewhere in our developing mind, someone told us that *hobbies don't pay the bills*, which is the biggest lie ever told! And so we live our lives, locking away our true desires, hoping that one day a perfect opportunity will come our way, and we finally will be able to showcase the gifts that God instilled in us.

But for now, so many choose to put the feeling of being alive on hold, Monday through Friday. Our children don't have that problem; they are pure, positive energy that chose to be here to show us the other side of life that we have forgotten or suppressed. If children mirror us, I want to be as playful as I can while making choices for my career and life that enhance my living experience daily.

About ten years ago, *Time* magazine did an article on a study of parents of happy, content, and successful adults. The results were mind-boggling to me. It was discovered that the biggest gift you can give your kids is not an education, material things, or advice (often unsolicited). It is an example of how to fully thrive and enjoy life to the fullest. The parents who lived their passion, loved their lives, and enjoyed the whole living experience had the most successful, happiest adult children!

I don't want my kids to think that making money should be a struggle or a sacrifice of fun. There are millions of people who live the best possible lives and make more money than those who struggle for it. If one's mind-set is developed in the early years, surely I can prevent my kids from having a mind-set that will propel them into a life where fun is reserved for vacations and weekends, a life where they are too busy working to have the lives they want to live and have no time to live the life they are working so hard for. I think that this generation is here to awaken us, teach us, and enhance the human race, not by conforming or following rules and guidelines that no longer suit these eager souls but by remaining true to who they were born to be. They are here to force us to do away with belief systems that no longer suit us and to explore other ideas with an open mind in hopes of evolving, not just revolving around the same mundane lifestyle.

Chapter 12

On April 16, just a few days before my due date, I woke up feeling unusually energized and felt compelled to clean every inch of my house. Like a bird preparing her nest for the arrival of a new addition, I made sure my house was spotless. It was a beautiful spring day, with the early feelings of warmth from the sun. I went outside for a really long walk—about four hours! With each step I told my boy how beautifully everything was blossoming, preparing for his arrival. The flowers were blooming, the grass was a juicy green, and birds were singing their hearts out all around us. I saw baby bunnies hopping around; I heard baby birds chirping. All of God's magnificent creations were coming alive, waking up after a sleepy winter.

I could smell change in the air. Spring had finally sprung, especially on that particular day, like no other day before. I called on my guardian angels, my grandmothers and Juliana, to help me welcome my son into the world. Thoughts of failing to have a natural birth didn't even enter my mind. I was already doing my gratitude prayers for a smooth, easy delivery. It was already so in my mind. As I walked, I felt him moving down my body. It felt so good, as he was off my diaphragm, and I was finally able to breathe deeply. I had a feeling something was happening, but I'd been down this road before. They say your labors get shorter every time, so I was ready for a two-day labor since my last one was four days. After dinner, I was so tired that the only way I could get the girls bathed was if we all took a bath together. As I lay in the tub, almost falling asleep, the girls drew a picture on my belly for their baby brother. The oily water crayon felt so good swirling on my belly. I dried us off, still with the picture on my belly, and we snuggled in my bed as I told them a story about two sisters who received a gift in the form of a baby brother. As they drifted off to sleep, I closed my eyes, holding Madelyn close to me. I felt the same emotions as I had when I'd held Milana on her last night as my only baby girl. I kept inhaling Madelyn's delicious scent and kissing her back as I wrapped my arms around her body. To me, she is God's light on this earth. The energy that consumed me when I was near her was euphoric. I looked at Milana as she lay sleeping and smiling, dreaming of all things beautiful. I prayed for them, thanking them for giving me so much love and for being so good to me when I was becoming increasingly tired and immobile in the last few days. I was grateful that I was the chosen one to bring these souls from heaven to earth. Consumed with feelings of love and light, I fell asleep around ten o'clock.

Within an hour, I woke up to an uncomfortable feeling in my abdomen; I felt my first contraction. I thought nothing of it and stayed in bed. Then a few minutes later, another contraction, then another, not slowing down but gaining strength. *Oh, my God! I am in labor!* I went downstairs to tell James what I was feeling. I contacted my Facebook friend to ask her what she thought of my symptoms. Amazingly, that entire day she'd seen me and the number seventeen in her mind. She said I was surely going to have the baby that very night. I contacted my mom, and she was at my house by midnight. The contractions were coming so fast and so strong that I could no longer pant through them. Shortly afterward, the cursing began—a sure sign that things were gaining momentum fast.

By 1:00 a.m., I was in the shower, trying to ease the pain. I checked myself, and I was about two centimeters dilated. I got a short break for about fifteen minutes and called my doctor to tell him I was in full-blown labor. The entire time, I remained calm, even making jokes between excruciating contractions. I felt safe in the arms of the universe, fully trusting that all would be well. We got dressed and headed for the hospital around 2:00 a.m. In the car, I was on my knees, hugging the backseat. As I rode the waves of contractions, the euphoric bliss of endorphins flooded every cell of my body. I prayed; I was so grateful to my body for its perfection and hard work and for giving me the gift of life once more. I thanked my son for being so strong and for coming to grace us with his presence. "The world is so magnificent. Come join us and enjoy it with us. We love you so much," I kept saying to my boy as I cradled my belly.

We arrived at the hospital around three o'clock. The pain was intense but still manageable. The nurses checked me and said I was almost six centimeters. In just four hours I had made so much progress. I was in awe of the perfection of my body. The doctor came in and instructed the anesthesiologist to give me an epidural in case of I needed an emergency C-section. This doctor was not like my previous one; he was an elderly man who did not support my desire for a vaginal delivery. He didn't deem it safe, and his nervous energy made my heart rate skyrocket. The baby wasn't too happy with him either because every time the doctor was in the room, the baby's heart rate would drop dramatically. My doctor didn't support my VBAC, but I didn't need his support; I just needed a doctor to deliver my baby. He stood over me with his negative, fearful energy, watching my contractions, showing James that it could be the beginning of uterine rupture.

I overheard the doctor tell James, "What are you doing? Let's stop this and get the baby out. He is not happy laboring with her." But the doctor did not scare James; he trusted me and my connection to my body.

I knew what signs to look for when the uterus begins to rupture, and what I was feeling was not that. I couldn't let his words seep in. I knew the baby was okay, and I felt that everything was progressing as it was supposed to. I fully trusted my instinct, and the doctor didn't scare me one bit. I asked him to turn the lights off and leave the room to give me a few minutes to stabilize the baby and myself.

During our many consultations he often told me stories of how fearful he is of deliveries. People who are consumed by fear will see a reason to panic at any given moment. If this had been the doctor who delivered Madelyn, I would fully trust in her judgment, as she always found a logical reason for everything. I needed to meditate, relax, and feel what was actually happening in my body, not what it looked like was happening on the monitor. He obliged and left the room.

As I lay still in the dark room, I felt my grandmother Alexandra, who had passed away a year prior, come over to me and help me. I could feel her rubbing my forehead, saying, "It's all going to be okay. Everything will be okay." It was so real to me; I even leaned my head toward her hand. My other grandmother Fanya, who passed away in 1996, was rubbing my feet, attempting to calm me down as well. I felt Juliana caress my belly, calming the baby down, raising his heart rate and making sure he was okay. I felt all the women who guided me and loved me from heaven right there with me, supporting me and assuring me they were beside me. As I surrendered to them with the utmost trust that all would be well, I was able to fall asleep. As I slept to the sensation of my grandmother's touch on my forehead, I felt one with two worlds—the real world and the dimension where my loved ones roamed. It was my first true meeting with them all at once—an awareness so real that no other thoughts could enter my mind. It was nothing short of bliss. Knowing I was cared for, just as I always felt when I was near them when they were alive, my body was able to fully relax.

Then as I fell into a deeper sleep and lost connection with them, I woke up to the monitors beeping. My body was shaking uncontrollably, and the baby's vitals began to dip again. The doctor ran in, turned the lights on, and begged me to reconsider the VBAC. I looked at James and his calm demeanor, still sleepy from his short nap, and it somehow slowed my shaking. The shaking was a side effect of the anesthesia from the epidural. At this point, I was at eight centimeters, and there was no way my body wouldn't finish the job. I asked the doctor to give me one more chance. I assured him that all would be well if he just calmed down and left me alone. It was now 5:30 a.m. I put myself back in the blissful embrace of my grandmothers and daughter. I took many deep breaths, talking to my son, asking him to calm down as I assured him that he would be in my arms very soon. I thanked my body over and over again for being so perfect, progressing so beautifully, and working so hard to finally give me my son, my dream, to hold. The more I trusted and let go, the better our vitals got. Within minutes of being still and being one with my angels, we were back to the perfect heart rate and oxygen levels.

I wondered what actually happened when a baby was brought into the world. Was he with God, who was preparing him to cross over into the real world? Were his own guiding angels here too, to assist him in the transition? Was I surrounded with my own angels and his? I felt my body fill with light as these beautiful thoughts consumed my mind. Then, I felt the baby's head push down, and I knew it was time to give birth. I called the nurse to tell her I was feeling a lot of pressure. She checked me, and sure enough, his head was in her hands! The doctor came in at 6:00 a.m. to prep me for delivery. As I had my legs in position and was ready to push, my contractions completely subsided. We waited and waited; nothing happened. For about ten minutes my legs were in stirrups, the light was shining on my glorious lady parts, and the doctor just stood there, waiting to catch the baby.

While we waited, the silence got a bit uncomfortable, so I decided to strike up a conversation. "Anyone have travel plans coming up? We going to Greece in three months for a wedding."

We talked about traveling and about the nurse's son's upcoming wedding. Then another doctor came in and looked at me in all my glory.

"Hi, my name is Katerina, and this is my husband James," I

said. James leaned in to shake his hand. It was like a conversation at a cocktail party—only not. It was so funny that we couldn't stop laughing. Suddenly, I felt the urge to push. I pushed once, took a deep breath, pushed again, took another deep breath, and pushed for the last time as the doctor said, "Congratulations! He is here."

Mason James was born at 6:18 a.m. on April 17 (exactly seven years and one month after Juliana passed away). Finally, my dream of holding my baby boy, my son, was a reality.

I was so grateful for all the angels who helped me get through a somewhat stressful labor. It was in that moment that I went from believing to having an undeniable "knowing" that I had guardians to take care of me. All they asked of me was to trust in them. It was a knowing that something else existed in the world besides what I could see and logically accept. I felt the strength of the world gather around me that day to make sure everything went as perfectly as it was designed to be. James and I kissed and then he left to go home and help my mom get the girls off to daycare. It was nice to be alone with the baby—no distractions, just us getting to know each other.

He was the most beautiful baby boy I had ever seen, and he looked exactly like Milana had when she was born. As I nursed him for the first time, he opened his eyes and looked directly at me. I couldn't stop smiling as my tears fell on his nose. I could feel his amazing aura, his beautiful light, pierce and merge with my soul. We were one from that moment to eternity. We snuggled all day. I inhaled his hair, and the softness of his hands caressed my face. This was it—the final puzzle piece to our family.

Throughout my pregnancy I'd always looked for signs, listening closely for angels to whisper the perfect name for our son. One day when I was about thirty weeks pregnant and on my way to the mall, I thought about the extraordinary journey we had been on from the day of his conception. I'd rebuilt my life, brick by brick, as he grew in my belly. We were together, creating the blueprint for my dream life. The word "build" kept coming up, and then it dawned on me—a mason is someone who works with stones. A mason builds structures, brick by brick, just like I was building my life. We also wanted to name all the kids with the letter M, mainly as a joke to play on James because he had Mommy, Milana, and Madelyn that he always kept confusing. It was also a miracle that we'd conceived any of our children, as they all sleep with us in one bed at least a few nights a week and certainly by 3:00 a.m., and the act of conception always was quite a challenge. Our son's middle name would honor his father, James. His middle initial, J, also would honor my father Jacob; James's father, Jeff; and our dearest Juliana—all the men in his life and his angel sister.

James, my parents, and the girls came to visit us at the hospital. Their faces, when they saw this perfect little piece of God's beauty, lit up with so much love. They wanted to hold him and kiss him. Though my parents were saying, "Don't touch him," I was all for it. "Touch him, bond with him, feel his amazing light, kiss him, and welcome him with all your heart into world," I said to them. He was the newest member of our family, and he was the newest friend to the girls. They squealed with joy as they held him and kissed him; they just couldn't get enough of him.

Madelyn and Milana jumped on my bed as I lay holding Mason, wanting to go to sleep all together and never wanting to leave. As we all snuggled, James put his arms around us all, and we had our first of many group hugs. It felt like the sky opened up to flood us with never-ending blessings and reasons to rejoice. My mom held Mason, and I saw her eyes water. She loved being a grandmother more than anything, and I was so happy to gift her with another grandchild. My dad put his arms around her, and they both stared at Mason. "Welcome to the world, our boy. We love you so much," my dad whispered as he kissed Mason's forehead.

Then James finally had a chance to hold him. I saw the excitement in his face as he said, "Hi, baby boy. Hello, my boy. Hi. I love you." James was going through a tough time at work, and it was as if Mason's light just brightened everything within him. I spent the next two days sleeping next to my boy, overwhelmed with gratitude for yet another gift. I kept saying, "Thank you for choosing me to be your mother. I am eternally grateful to you for the gift of your presence in my life."

On the day when we finally came home, I went into the living room to call the girls for dinner. I walked in the room, and my heart almost exploded. Milana had put Mason on her chest and sat with him, facing the window, which displayed a stunning sunset. Their faces were still, peaceful, and engulfed in the sun's golden rays. I grabbed the camera and took a picture before they saw me.

Milana noticed me and said, "We are saying thank you to the sun. I am showing Mason what we do here at sunset since it's his first day here with us."

I felt tears coming down; I was so proud of her and was so happy that she too found bliss in sunset gratitude prayers. Our family felt complete with Mason's finally joining us; the girls couldn't keep their hands off him and wanted to always find a reason to help me with him. Madelyn, then a little over two years old, was our main diaper-changer. Whether it was poop or pee, she would wipe him until he was spotless, often using about a hundred wipes. It was okay; the big-sister pride she felt was amazing. Milana had a magic touch; when Mason would cry, she would pick him up and sing him a song. Often, she would make it up as she went along. "Hush, little baby brother. I love you so. Your cute little nose is the cutest of all. I'm your sister, and I'll teach you how to play, never letting anyone stand in your way. The sun is gone, but the moon is out, and Mommy has to give you boobies so you grow up big." Her perfectly soothing voice and her gentle dance worked almost instantly; he was in awe of her.

It's no wonder the most successful, happiest people on the planet exhibit childlike behavior—inquisitive but not judgmental, seeing the world through innocence, always assuming the best in everyone and everything. I often wonder at what point in our lives we begin to frown more than we smile, work more than we play, have more focus than seeing the whole picture, or feel more frustration than flowing with the river of life, changing shape with ease, according to each situation.

Before I go on, let me clarify my understanding of God. God is the source of everything; it is the light in all that's dark, and it is the energy that thrives off love and joy. Perhaps it's because the little ones are still one with God and one with his light that shines within them that it is so blissful to look at them and be around them. It's evident in their eyes. I can see God manifesting himself when I stare at a child's face. Maybe that's why they see good in everything. Their eyes don't judge; they see everything as it is—purely magical.

I considered this thought when I realized that the further I was from the God within me, the more I felt compelled to judge others and situations in a negative light. I felt so empty, dark, and hollow; there was no light. There was no God residing within me. I felt like God was above me, watching me, and judging me, but he wasn't one with me. We were two separate entities, trying to work together to no avail. I feared him. I saw him as something outside of me, and that was my biggest pitfall.

I watched many videos that professed that the only way to God was to be one with him. It was only when I merged with his energy and light that I began to see through his eyes. I saw what he sees in me. I saw what he sees in others around me, and I saw what he sees in the simplicity of nature around us. When I was separate from God, the only way for me to feel superior to another person was to judge that person and think I was better than he is, even if for a second. However, the closer I merged with the light of God, the more I was blessed with the ability to see him in others as well. My world began to fill with magnificent beings. Everywhere I went I saw his light—in the smile of a young kid pumping my gas, an elderly man whose cart rolled over my foot at the grocery store, the violent child who was throwing a fit at the mall. Suddenly, I could no longer see anger or even the clothing others were wearing, I saw them for their best selves that reside deep within their souls. I no longer saw color, race, religious beliefs, or even gender. I saw people for the light they were emitting from their souls. I saw that all our desires are the same—to be loved and understood and to experience joy. Suddenly, people stopped cutting me off (maybe they still did, but I just didn't realize it). People stopped upsetting me (maybe they still did, but I just didn't see it that way).

The oldest monk at the Tibetan monastery said that the glue that holds the entire universe together is compassion.

I am finally living in the same world with those peaceful beings that I saw exactly a year ago in Florida. I am no longer judging my dreams or myself as a mother, wife, or daughter. I am following my gut—my knowing that was always there—but my logical and fearful self would try desperately to disregard my own truth. The more I suppressed my knowing, which I realize now was God's attempt to communicate with me, the worse I felt.

Whenever we have a gut instinct, that's God trying to tell us something is wrong and needs to be addressed. Most of us run from our anxiety-ridden feelings—I know I did—and this is the main cause of so much pain in our lives. Women are especially intuitive. We somehow know exactly what we desire, but the never-ending voices of advice from those we love interferes with our own voices. We are often left anxious and confused about the course we need to take when it comes to our marriages, our children, and our own lives. The more voices we allow to permeate our thoughts, the harder it is to hear what our hearts are trying to say.

For every *want* our hearts have, there are ten thousand *shoulds* our minds create. Once we begin on the journey to unveil our eyes and raise the volume of our truth, we begin to soar. I told this story earlier, but it bears repeating: the Jewish explanation of our intuition holds a lot of merit. Before we are born, we are told everything that will happen to us throughout our lives. Shortly before we come in to the world, an angel touches our upper lips, leaving a dent, and that does not make communication easy until we are well over two years old. By then, we have already mostly forgotten our conversation with the angel and are now ready to pursue a life to figure out what our purpose is. We live in a state of amnesia, though once in a while our memories of what our purposes are surface in the form of intuition or gut instinct. Since the angel told us what our purpose is, it is recorded within our souls. Our job is to spend our life coming out of amnesia and living a life "on purpose," with a purpose.

I believe that before we come into the world, we are gifted with angels who help us discover our reason for being here. They make everything easy and possible when we pursue our purpose and everything hard and a struggle when we ignore our intuitive desire to seek the reason we are here. We spend our lives with a knowing of what is right, and often the solution lies within us, within our hearts and souls. Our life's purpose is to bring forth the knowledge that was forgotten because it was never lost. Our knowing is our destiny, and it throws down a rope so that we spend our days climbing upward to understand and experience the true bliss in which we were born to bask. Anxiety is the nudge we get from our intuition; it's seeking our action. It wants to be heard, and the harder we try to shush it, the louder it gets. Often, it manifests itself in chest pains, stomach pains, and anxiety attacks. Just because you don't chose to listen to your gut, it doesn't mean it will give up on trying to be heard. Save yourself the stress and pain, and listen … and then act. It's the only way to make the pain go away. Often the action itself is much easier and more liberating than the fear of knowing you must act but are choosing not to do so.

One of the most profound changes that I experienced within myself was my relationship with my body. Since I was a little girl, most of the wishes I made when I blew out my birthday candles were to be thin. I was never overweight, but I did have a pudgy body. It didn't help when a crush told me, "You have a beautiful face, but if you can just narrow your body you would be perfect."

That phrase stuck with me for so many years. When I was about twenty-one, another crush mine said when we were at the beach, "That woman has five kids. Look at her flawless body. It's amazing."

I was impressed with the woman who looked so toned as her

children ran around her. I thought she was a goddess, able to defy the odds of pregnancies ruining her body for life. I swore to myself that when I had children, no matter how many, I would do everything in my power to maintain my body. Things didn't really work out that way, though I still look pretty good after having four kids.

While I was pregnant I had crazy cravings for pizza, but I thought of what it would do to my body. As I got bigger, I got more scared of how I would ever get my body back. Then, after giving birth to my daughter, I was so happy that my body was capable of perfectly creating this gorgeous human being. But as feelings of gratitude toward my body wore off, it was time to have a talk with myself about how I was going to get my body back.

Honestly, if anyone would ever speak to me the way I speak to me, I would probably be in jail for my violent outburst. I would look in the mirror and watch my sagging abdomen stare back at me. *Ugh, how am I ever going to lose this ugly belly? I can't believe how fat I am. I am never eating again!* Months would go by, and my weight slowly began to go down, but I was far from the goddess I saw on the beach with her five children. While Juliana was sick, I didn't have much time to think about my body or its imperfections. And during the time I was grieving, my weight went up and down, depending on the severity of my sadness. After getting pregnant with Milana, I watched very closely what I ate. Luckily, I was so poor that I could barely afford more food than I needed. After giving birth to Milana, I felt enormous gratitude for my body for giving me yet another gift from God. After few months and daily two-hour walks, my body was slowly coming back around, but again, it was far from the goddess I saw on the beach.

I was so focused on what I saw in the mirror that I completely disregarded what I saw within me. It took me more than two years to finally get back to my pre-pregnancy (number two) weight. Interestingly, the last ten pounds were lost almost instantly when my milk supply began to significantly dwindle. I didn't know at the time that my body was holding on to fat so that my milk supply would be ample enough to keep feeding Milana. I thought my body was pretty incredible but again, I didn't fully understand how magnificent it really was. All I knew for sure was that my body was not the fat-burning machine it once was.

Almost to the day that I lost the baby weight from Milana—she was two and a half—I got pregnant with Madelyn. My pregnancy was absolutely perfect with her, as it was with my previous babies. I don't know how much weight I gained, but I looked and felt amazing. It wasn't until I was on a mission to view my body as perfection so that I could successfully deliver her vaginally that I really began to understand the miracle that my body is. After giving birth to Madelyn I was in complete awe of my body's capabilities. I couldn't believe the perfection of it. It not only conceived, grew, nourished, and then delivered my baby, but it then flooded my breasts with nature's perfect food to keep my baby alive, thriving, and safe from sickness. It grew a human being virtually "hands free"—I did nothing to assist it. All it needed was nourishment. I felt so close to my body; we established a bond that can only measure up to a bond created in the trenches of war. We beat the odds and survived a VBAC after two C-sections. *Wow, my body is amazing!*

Weight loss was slow, but I was fortunate to have the means to afford high-quality food. Though I didn't lose the weight right away, I did manage it. I would look in the mirror and think to myself, *What a stunning body I have, not bad for having three babies,* But again, not the goddess I saw on the beach. Only after I began to focus on getting to know the soul that was housed by the body I saw in the mirror did the weight melt away, about eighteen months after giving birth. Almost to the day that I hit my pre-Juliana-pregnancy weight, I got pregnant with Mason. I even made a joke on Facebook: "Today I am 4 ounces away from my pre-pregnancy weight … expect a baby announcement shortly!"

My boy wanted nothing but pizza and sandwiches all day, every day. I was completely at his service and gave in to all my "carbo-licious" cravings. I knew I would gain weight as I always did, but this time I was more attached to the woman I wanted to be than the woman I saw at the beach. I knew I would lose it all if I chose to make changes in my diet and exercise regimen. I was so in love with my body for growing yet another gift from God that I did not allow any negative thoughts toward it to enter my mind. Again, I was so consumed and focused on my inner growth that the exterior growth of my belly (and arms, and thighs, and back fat) was not getting any attention.

To me, I still looked good. How can you look bad when you are growing a miracle inside you? How can you utter any kind of negative words toward the body that is the single portal that brings souls from heaven to earth? For the first time in my life, I felt an enormous amount of respect and adoration for my body, not in passing as I had before but in the very depth of my heart. After giving birth, I couldn't help but flood my daily thoughts with gratitude toward it for giving me the privilege for the fourth time to be a mother again. Though the weight loss has been slow, I refuse to go on a diet. I refuse to feed myself junk food, not because I fear gaining weight but because I am worthy of the best food in the world.

When I switched my thinking from watching my diet for vanity reasons to watching my diet for reasons of love for my body, the results became amazing. Not a day goes by that I don't thank my body for being so perfect and healthy that my children have a mother one more day. I am so grateful for its perfection and that I am able to live out my dreams with energy and vitality. Maybe I feel this way because I am so in awe of the nonphysical part of me that I have little energy left to focus on the physical aspect of me, which isn't even me; it just houses the real me.

I am not my body. I am not my weight. I am a force of love and joy. I listen to what my body wants, and I give it what it asks with little judgment for it's requests. If my body wants carbs, I give it carbs. If my body wants something sweet, I give it something sweet. But because my body is in a state of joy, the law of attraction is attracting healthy, wholesome food. If you feel like shit, you will, by the law of attraction, attract shitty food. If you feel alive, you will attract food that continues making you feel alive! These days, I do T25 (a twenty-five-minute workout video of intense cardio) every morning and can't wait to get my body in the shape it deserves!

I want to talk about something that is very important to me and I believe to many people on this earth: freedom. Millions of people die for the sake of preserving it and living in it. When I began to understand what freedom really is, I made it my life goal to truly experience it in every aspect of my life. I exercised freedom when I was designing my dreams, never allowing limiting thoughts to plague my visions, though it was my biggest battle with myself. I exercised freedom within my own marriage. Where I formerly would keep my mouth shut for fear of sharing my thoughts or feelings for the purpose of preserving my own image, I was now fearlessly sharing all I wanted to say. Regardless of the consequences that sharing my inner deepest feelings would bring (an argument or judgment), I stopped arguing with James in my thoughts and began to write him letters, expressing my deepest emotions. That's when I began to feel the light within me. I encouraged James to share his inner feelings and assured him I wouldn't judge, no matter how wrong they were in my opinion. When we began to communicate more freely, we grew closer together and felt compassionate toward each other rather than resentment. That is when we truly became one. Where I used to see anger, I saw a man trying desperately to be heard, loved, understood, and appreciated. When two people can openly and—more importantly—freely be their truest selves within the relationship, amazing connections within the soul begin to take place.

Communication is key to everything within the marriage. I know it's a cliché that so many long-term couples say, but it holds an enormous amount of merit.

Today, I practice freedom of my true expression on a daily basis without fear of judging myself or being judged. I found that people judge others on the exact same level as they judge themselves. I realize that the judgment comes from their own struggle within themselves, and so I don't take it personally. It's actually quite liberating, once you acknowledge this concept.

To understand your life, you must first understand the power of your thoughts. Once you understand how powerful you are by seeing how many negative circumstance in life you brought on, imagine the amazing circumstances you can bring to your life by using the same technique that brought you negative ones. Look around your life from an objective point of view; it is the direct reflection of your inner thoughts and feelings. Change your thoughts, feelings, and life. All that you want is there when you look up and think up. All that you don't want is down, when you think down. Live in love, all day every day. Live in gratitude for all that you have. If you don't have much, begin with little things.

Your body is functioning perfectly right now, giving your children a parent to make memories with and receive guidance from. Imagine the pain they would feel if you were to die; it would be so heartbreaking. Now that you see a contrast, feel the joy and gratitude for being alive. We live in amazing times; if we chose to learn or change anything in our lives we have access to more information than ever before. We live in such a free world where we can chose to change our lives and have tools to assist us, often without leaving our homes or spending money.

Be grateful to be born during an era like the one we are living now. You have full power to change and design your life, starting from the little things that irk you to the massive things that nourish you. Since I began to fully accept the fact that my life is a reflection of my thoughts, I feel so empowered. When things go wrong, I don't take it personally. I ask myself, "Where did I lose my thoughts on this situation?" Of course things happen unexpectedly. Other people make choices for themselves that sometimes directly affect us. However, I will never give up the power that I have, which is to choose how I respond to my circumstances.

Our lives should not be one stressful event. Life gives us the gift of contrast; you can't see light unless you're in a dark space. You can't feel love unless you once felt a lack of it or the pain of feeling hate. After a severe cold or flu, do you wake up after days of feeling like hell and feel like you want to hug the world because you feel so good? The only way to experience a true breakthrough is to first go to the bottom of life's pit. Until you are so sick of yourself, your life, your thoughts, and all the negativity, you can't fully experience the truest gift of bliss. That is reserved only for those who realize that they don't really know anything and are ready to listen, to do anything but continue living the life they live.

Things should always work out if you expect them to. Luck should be your best friend if you expect it to be. Love should fuel your life if you expect it to. Money should come easily and abundantly if you expect it to. Your children should be their very best if you expect them to be. You spouse should be loving, caring, and understanding of you, if you expect him to be. But don't expect it while feeling hope as you cross your fingers. Truly and fully expect it to be so. The positivity that your expectations will be met needs to be emitted to the universe in order for it to come to fruition. Look around your life at the things you want to change. What are they mirroring to you about your inner world? Take back full control of your addiction to fearful thoughts, unworthy emotions, and low expectations. Take back your mind. Don't allow it to roam where it wants to go.

I keep thinking about the kind of world I want to create for my children. Everything begins at home. What if we instill beliefs in our children that the world is a beautiful place, filled with life that is created by the same Creator who creates everything, and we are the co-creators. What if we create a generation of human beings who live in freedom to express who they truly are, without fear of judgment or disappointment to others? Isn't the root of all evil the lack of self-expression and the lack of living from the heart, soul, and intuition? We focus on educating our children to think logically. Is logic really the best way to think? Isn't logic the killer of all dreams?

Isn't logic the cause of so much misalignment with who we really are? How about living from a place of knowing, a place of trusting one's intuition. All those shining in our society are doing so not because of logic but because of a burning desire to give their gifts and share their ideas with the world.

It's horrible to realize all the blood that was shed over religious beliefs. Only those who are lost convert the most beautiful words of God into acts of horror.

If we instill beliefs in ourselves and in our children that living from the heart is the only way to live, there won't be any depression or anxiety. Depression and anxiety are a chemical imbalance manifested when the being of a person becomes detached from the source (God), which compelled the human cells to divide with the intention of creating a perfect human being at conception. You are absolutely perfect. You are God's greatest creation. Though it's hard to believe, it is the absolute truth. The more aligned you get with the source of all, the more you will see yourself through the eyes of perfection. Everything you ever wanted to be, you are. You just have to bring forth that light from within to shine brighter for the world to see. As you begin to shine, you will blind all those around you, who will no longer care to see what you are trying to be but what you truly are.

When we lose trust in the source, the Creator, God or light, that is when we are plagued by worry because we feel alone. We feel detached and often hopeless. Loneliness is the lowest of all human emotions, and it can't exist in a person who is one with her true self and is guided by her intuition.

This concept was the hardest for me to understand and accept, I am used to controlling everything around me. Surely it's easier to control others than it is to control ourselves. Solutions to other people's problems are so clear to us but are blurry when it comes to our own problems. However, the more I took control of the world within me, the faster the world around me took care of itself, working out flawlessly and effortlessly. You will no longer feel compelled to hold your life and all those in it by the throat, desperate to control. You will let go of the grip and allow the energy that perfectly created you to guide you, protect you, and love you. There will no longer be feelings of "something is missing." You will be whole and pursue all you desire with absolute certainty that it will work out, even if you have no idea how.

Think back on your life. How many amazing things have happened unexpectedly? They happened because you gave up control and just flowed with the stream. Follow your bliss; forget the saying, "Not everything is about pleasure." It is; you are here to experience the highest forms of pleasure. Why else would the energy of life compel your parents to make love on the particular day they conceived you? (They made love many times before, but conception didn't take place.) You had to be born; you had to be here; and your job is to figure out why.

All the answers lie within you, if you can shush the voices that are coming from outside of you long enough to hear what your soul is telling you. Your job is to raise your attraction level to all that you desire. Happiness is the only way. The more I was in control of my thoughts, the more I was able to direct my thinking to my present experience—my now moment. I understood one very important aspect of thought: a negative thought that causes anxiety within me is a direct communication from my soul, asking me to address a particular situation before it becomes a bigger problem. It feels as if the universe was created with the hope that all those within it would be in total control of their minds, their lives, and their happiness.

These days I don't allow thoughts of worry or fear to enter my mind. I'm very different from the person I was throughout my life. Maybe it's because I come from a family of worriers. Most of my thoughts were driven by fear in an attempt to control the people and circumstances around me. I kept failing miserably, but I didn't know how to stop. They would just start with one tiny worry, and by 3:00 a.m., they would snowball into "World War III is coming" fears by sunrise. That's not me anymore and never will be. I live in full trust that I was put on this earth with the greatest force of love. It will not let me down. Yes, there will be hard times ahead, but with God's light engraved in every cell of my body, I will persevere. Nothing is terminal ... and if it is, so be it.

A really fun game I play is to envision my thoughts as a horse race. Sometimes, I get on a thought-horse that doesn't feel good. As soon as I get the feeling, I say, "Oh no, I am getting off this horse. Not going to ride in to the night on this one." I make a joke out of it, but it really works. I now worry productively. All my negative thoughts are addressed, and action is taken immediately. If the negative thought is irrational, then I am not going to waste my amazing mind on thinking of it when I have so many more bliss-producing thoughts waiting. No longer do I waste perfectly magical moments on worry of what may or may not happen. Some might think I am living in la-la land, but I am actually living in more reality than when I was a worrier, which is a skewed reality anyway.

I don't take life so seriously; it's just a game, and whoever masters it wins. Think of a video game. There are many different levels and all kinds of scary characters with guns coming at you, but you can only move up in levels if you learn the proper way to respond to all that comes at you. That takes hours and hours of playing the game until you master the right responses to all the bad guys. Life is all about moving up in levels. Our experiences will either destroy us or let us move on to the next level. The good news is that as you move up in levels, it gets better, easier, and more interesting.

Now I understand how intertwined we all are. Just think how many times you picked up the phone to call someone, and that person called you at that moment. A technique I came up with is to visualize a bubble around my children in my mind. I pour all my love and support in that bubble, filling it with light.

Every time a fearful or anxious thought enters your mind about a particular person, bring your thoughts back to visualizing the bubble of love and light. This is most effective way to protect them from negative influences and circumstances. When you send emotions of worry or fear to them, those are not protective forces; they can actually harm them. This is especially powerful from a mother to a child. As a mother worries, the cells in her heart begin to react to her emotional being at the moment. At the same time, she sends that negative, fearful energy to the cells of her child's body. You can do this with everything you worry about. If it's holding on to your job, send that love to your boss or clients.

A Russian scientist did an experiment to determine how fast and far our love can travel. To his dismay, there are no boundaries. When someone sends love to another person he loves, you can see the cells in the receiver's heart reacting instantly. I used to worry about not having enough money; now I know money is always going to find its way into my account—and it has. I used to worry about my marriage; now I know what fucks marriages up is the lack of freedom to communicate from the soul. Of course, my marriage still requires a lot of work, and I am more than willing to give it what it needs. And when I can no longer do so, then I will have to make a choice. But I refuse to live in denial, silence, helplessness, or powerlessness. I am more real than ever before. Statistics and logic don't scare me anymore. I learned that when you live your life from a brain the size of a pea, your view on the world is the same size. When you live your life from the massive size of your being, you see the world in all its glory.

Media no longer scares me. I understand that it's their hope to make us live in fear so that we gladly relinquish our freedom for the sake of a falsified temporary feeling of safety. I used to read about politics; now I only read about unusual human acts of kindness, love, and compassion. We are all different but share one desire; that is, to be happy, loved, understood, and accepted as we are. I no longer feel threatened by those whose actions I can't understand. I am no longer interested in judging others. Let's all unite our families in love and compassion. Let's live our lives with freedom to express our truth, not allowing beliefs that no longer serve us to control our choices.

Let's shush the voices around us and listen closely to the voice within us. It somehow already knows exactly how to make us our happiest.

Whatever feels good, follow it. Whatever makes you happy, keep doing it. Whatever leaves you in awe, keep looking at it. Bring all that gives you joy into your life and focus on it. What you focus on grows; grow all the happiness in your life that you know, deep down inside, you are worthy of receiving. You will begin to attract more bliss than you ever thought possible.

Let's focus our attention on being authentic, not on being who we hope others perceive us to be. Let's live from our hearts and leave our minds to do the job of keeping us alive, not making us feel as if were dead. Let's support the good in us and abandon the bad. Let's not judge ourselves so harshly but fill our souls with love of ourselves.

My reason for writing this book was to bring light to ideas for parents to consider. If I can help manifest happier mothers, then surely I can help create happy adults with whom my children can share the world. This is my way of giving my children a world I dream of.

As Dr. Dyer once said, "Change the way you look at things, and the things you look at will begin to change." I promise you that!

About the Author

Katerina Mayants was born in Belarus on February 15, 1983 to two incredibly loving parents and an amazing older brother. In 1991, she migrated to Brooklyn New York. Today, she lives in New Jersey with her 3 beautiful children, two cats and wonderful husband in a peaceful suburban town.

63807111R00123

Made in the USA
Middletown, DE
05 February 2018